Sunshine & Sass

Ellen Brooks

Editor: Brynn Paulin

Cover Design: Matador Designs

click. read. relish.

Join my newsletter today.

www.ellenbrooks.info/newsletter

Three chords and the truth

That's what a country song is

~ Willie Nelson

The Welcome to Kissing Springs Collection

Read all 24 books across 3 seasons by multiple authors.

Santa Season
Welcome to Kissing Springs

Sunshine Season
Welcome to Kissing Springs: Sunshine Season

Bourbon Season
Welcome to Kissing Springs: Bourbon Season

Visit **www.kissingsprings.com** for everything Kissing Springs!

Contents

December | Atlanta 1

1. Macy 3
2. Cole 9
3. Macy 13
4. Cole 17
5. Macy 19
6. Cole 25
7. Macy 29

New Year's Eve | Kissing Springs 33

8. Cole 35
9. Macy 39
10. Cole 45
11. Macy 51
12. Cole 57

Valentine's Day | Nashville 63

13. Macy 65
14. Cole 71
15. Macy 77
16. Cole 83

17. Macy 89
18. Macy 95
March | New York City 99
19. Cole 101
20. Macy 107
21. Cole 115
22. Macy 119
23. Cole 123
24. Macy 127
25. Cole 133
July | Kissing Springs 139
26. Macy 141
27. Cole 147
28. Macy 153
29. Cole 159
30. Macy 165
Epilogue | Cole | The Next Morning 173
Also By Ellen Brooks 179
About the Author 183

December | Atlanta

You say you love me and its inviting,
to go where life is more exciting
But I was raised on country sunshine
~ Country Sunshine by Dottie West

1

Macy

My hair's a frizzy mess, my stomach is still protesting the turbulence from the flight, and I can picture exactly where I left my grandmother's lucky bracelet on the bathroom counter at home, but the worst part of my day is right now.

I glance at the clock on the dash of the town car and grit my teeth. I'm over an hour behind schedule, and I hate running late. Especially today, when I'm slated to fill in as the opening act on a country superstar's nationwide tour.

I roll my neck, but the unyielding knots refuse to loosen. My shoulder blades are so tight I can just imagine them fusing together. After all, this is the chance of a lifetime. A dream come true.

Tonight, I'll be performing on a stage in a sold-out stadium for tens of thousands of people. Opening for Heartwood, a band so popular it's held the number one spot on the charts for fourteen weeks and hasn't fallen out of the top one hundred since their debut album three years ago.

To say tonight might give a much needed shot in the arm to my career, which has been limping along for the past five years, is an understatement. I've got to be flawless.

And I need to put out of my mind that I've left my five-year-old, who I've never spent a night away from since he was born, with his father and my cousin, Hannah, for a few days back in my small hometown.

The town car driver deposits me and my suitcase at the back entrance of the concert venue. I stomp the dirty gray slush off my boots as one of the two beefy security guards checks my driver's license and radios in to confirm I'm okay to admit.

It takes at least ten minutes to get the all clear. I spend that time rocking back and forth on my heels and biting my lip, but finally, he holds open the door so I can slip inside, out of the freezing December afternoon, and nods toward the stage. "They're doing sound check now."

Backstage is a flurry of activity, and I stop the first person who looks somewhat official, makes eye contact with me, and doesn't have their hands full.

"Hi, I'm looking for Ben Stuart."

The man dips his chin toward the sound booth set up on the floor of the stadium. "He's in the booth but will be back once Cole finishes up."

Cole Heartwood, he means. Lead singer and country heart-throb. A man known for his amazing vocals, drop-dead gorgeous smile, and infamous playboy reputation.

"They're almost done. You can wait over there." The man nods toward an alcove at the side of the stage before rushing away.

"Thank you," I call after him, though chances are good he couldn't hear me over the commotion.

The first notes of one of Heartwood's most popular songs sound throughout the empty arena, and I stop to watch from the shadows. Cole is center stage at the microphone with his famous mahogany acoustic guitar and his even more famous snug, low-slung jeans.

The rest of the band is in place onstage, but there are also a dozen children fanned out in a semi-circle behind the star. They join in on the chorus, their medley of youthful voices full of passion. I blink away the tears that prick the back of my eyes as their little lungs give it their all, and I miss my son, Mason, hundreds of miles away, even more.

When the song finishes, Cole spins to face the kids. "That was perfect, guys, really. I tell you what, you sing your hearts out again just like that tonight under the bright lights and you'll steal the show. The folks that fill these seats will give you the loudest applause of your lives, trust me. The crowd will walk away and say, man, Heartwood was great, but those children really brought the soul."

The kids erupt into excited chatter as a stagehand takes Cole's guitar and a woman wearing an Atlanta Children's Choir shirt emerges from the other side of the stage and holds up a camera. "Cole, how about a picture with the kids?"

"Of course, happy to," he says as the rest of the band pull out their earpieces and make their way offstage.

Cole is still posing for photos and signing autographs for the kids when a man's voice calls out my name from behind me. "Macy? Macy Porter?"

I spin to find Ben Stuart, one of the best known managers in Nashville, immediately recognizable thanks to his ginger hair and matching thick beard.

"Yes, hi. It's nice to meet you."

I thrust out a hand, which he shakes, meeting my eyes with a smile that puts me at ease. Or as *at ease* as I can be at this moment.

"I'm glad you could fill in for a few days on such short notice. We really appreciate it."

"I'm thrilled to be here."

"Ready for sound check? We're running a little late because of the kids but need to get out of here so the tech crew can finish up. Are you mic'd up?"

"Not yet."

"Let's get that taken care of," he says, glancing around. "Then you can get out there and get a feel for the stage. I'll grab Cole for the run-through of the duet, too, before he takes off."

"Duet?"

Ben's gaze snaps back to me. "Yeah, you know when the opener comes out later on during the show to perform with the headliner?"

"I know what you mean." I shake my head and attempt to rein in the racing thoughts that are quickly spiraling to panic. "I just didn't know I would be doing that since I'm only filling in for two nights."

"Well, if you don't want to—"

"No," I exclaim, grabbing his arm. "I'd... I'd be happy to. I didn't practice, but I'm sure I'll be fine. You said we'll do a run-through, right?"

I swallow hard and hope I don't sound half as panicky as I feel. I need to appear every bit the experienced professional they hired, not some one-hit wonder who doesn't know what the hell they're doing.

He places a reassuring hand on mine and nods. "Yes, a run-through in about five minutes."

Five minutes.

Rather than reveal the alarm manifesting as adrenaline racing through my veins, I shrug and nod. "Sounds great."

Ben introduces me to a member of the sound tech crew, who connects a power pack and microphone to the waistband of my jeans and runs a wire up the back of my shirt.

From where we stand, Cole, who's still onstage, is in my direct line of sight. He seems to have taken care of every picture and autograph request and clears his throat to address the group one last time. At least three kids elbow or shush their friends, who don't fall silent right away.

"Thanks again for helping us out tonight at the show. I can't wait to have you all onstage with me and the rest of the band. And if music is your dream, your passion, believe in yourself and work hard. Keep practicing and take advantage of every opportunity that comes your way because there are plenty of fans out there ready to sing along to a song you'll write, or sing, or play one day."

As they chorus goodbye, he heads off stage in the other direction. My brow furrows. The Cole Heartwood I expected doesn't square up with the man encouraging these young singers.

"Everything okay?" Ben asks, catching sight of my face as he returns to my side.

"Yeah, I just... Never mind."

I shake off my confusion and try to focus, but Ben tips his head in Cole's direction. "He's not one to mince words. If there's one thing you can count on with Cole, it's that he means exactly what he says."

My eyes trail back toward where Cole departed a moment ago. Maybe, his honesty and kindness aren't as newsworthy as his wicked grin or his love 'em and leave 'em reputation.

"Good to know."

"And you're good to go." Ben gives me an encouraging smile. "They're ready for you up front."

I step onto the stage and take my place in the bright lights at the center microphone Cole vacated only minutes ago. A disembodied voice crackles in my earpiece.

"Ms. Porter, are you ready? Let's hear just you before we add music, okay? Give us just a minute."

I drag in a lungful of air and release it slowly, praying this sound check goes off without a hitch.

2

Cole

"You feeling good? Everything sounded great with the kids."

Ben, my manager, who's more like a protective older brother, claps me on the back as I take a swig of water.

"Yeah, I think so." I reach around and unhook the mic pack, but he stops me.

"Before you do that, you've got to run through the—"

But he's cut off as a voice sounds throughout the auditorium. I can't see the front of the stage, but a woman's voice—soft and tentative at first—gains confidence and grows louder as she sings an a capella rendition of a song I've never heard.

It must be an original, but the words don't even register. Hell, they don't even matter. It's her arresting tone, unique range, and breathy pitch that halts me in my tracks. It's a voice with a rare quality that stands out, even in Nashville.

Ben's watching me, worry creasing his brow, and mutters, "Told you I'd find someone to fill in."

Our opener for this national holiday tour caught the flu three days ago, in Austin, or maybe it was Dallas. Either way, he's out of commission, and whoever this woman is, she's talented. Very talented.

"You did and she's good, so why the frown?"

He shoots me a familiar look, his jaw clenching. "I've met her."

"And..." I raise my eyebrows and trail off, waiting for his explanation.

He sighs and shakes his head. "Wait 'til you see her."

I spin toward the stage, curiosity drawing me as much as the lilting melody and her bluesy undertone. She's holding back. Anyone with half an ear can tell.

Standing in the shadows, I watch as she leans in on the chorus, gripping the microphone with both hands, her feet planted and her long, dark curls swaying. She's wearing tight jeans and sturdy, fur-trimmed, brown winter boots.

I'm no songwriter, but this one seems to have been written for her or maybe by her. It takes advantage of her natural ability and highlights her best features.

The jumbotrons flicker to life and, after a second, it's her face that fills the screens. A gorgeous face with bright blue eyes and rosy pink lips.

"Her name's Macy, Macy Porter. She's out of Nashville," Ben says, stepping up to my side.

Macy belts out the last line of the song. She's found her footing and is giving it all she's got. You'd think there was a sold-out crowd filling the stadium instead of empty seats and a handful of stagehands setting up equipment all around her. Her eyes squeeze shut as the final note fills my ears and reverberates in my chest.

"There you go," I murmur, my admiration for her vocals quickly falling to the more insistent desire to know everything about this breathtaking woman.

"I want to give her a song or two to warm up, but then you'll need to run through the duet with her."

"Happy to."

Ben runs a hand through his hair. "I had a feeling you'd say that."

"What?" I ask, picking up on the defeat in his voice.

"Don't get any ideas, Cole."

I shot him a sidelong smile. "Me, ideas?"

"Cleaning up your reputation is already a full-time job, and I'd prefer not to have to hire another PR specialist. They don't come cheap, especially for a client like you."

"So bill me."

"Believe me, we do. Macy's just filling in for two nights. She'll be on a plane back to Nashville first thing Friday morning."

"Sounds perfect."

"Why did I have a feeling that's what you were going to say?"

"Because," I say, thrusting my half-empty water bottle against his chest, "You're the best manager there is."

"I'm the only manager that will put up with your shit is what you mean."

I clap him on the shoulder and flash him one of my most dazzling smiles. "That, too, and I love you for it."

3

Macy

"You've got quite the pipes."

I spin around at the familiar voice, low and husky, only inches behind me. Cole Heartwood sidles up to my side with a second microphone stand and sets it down a foot from mine.

"Um, thanks."

"Cole, Cole Heartwood." He thrusts out a hand. "Glad to have you here."

He's not as tall in person as I would have thought, but still eclipses me by a good six inches. I look up and meet his observant dark eyes, but it's the whisper of a smile I can't help but study.

Finally, I drag my attention back to the man and away from his sinful lips and shake his hand. "Macy Porter. It's nice to meet you."

"That an original?" he asks, and it takes a second to realize he's asking about the song I just sang.

"Yeah, wrote it myself."

He cocks his head and lowers his voice. "Singer and songwriter, a lethal combination."

He's a lethal combination. When I don't answer, he continues. "Down from Nashville for just a couple of days, from what I hear."

"Yeah, just filling in."

Still holding my hand, he leans in so close I smell his cologne. Or maybe, it's just expensive soap. Either way, it's earthy with an essence that's both fresh and clean. But also unmistakably masculine and somehow sexy. "Well then, I'd better make the most of these few days."

The undertone in his voice is delicious. Hell, he's barely said a handful of words, and yet, here I am, mesmerized. This man's a born charmer—with years of honing his skills—and boy, does he know it. I'd be best off to steer clear. Unfortunately, other parts of my body, lower and less discriminating, sing a different tune.

Despite my resolve and against my better judgment, I return his sultry smile. "Me, too."

He cocks an eyebrow and hooks his thumb into the pockets of his jeans, and I can tell he knows I'm not talking about the music, either.

"He really knows how to put on a show, hmm?"

"He sure does."

I meet Ben's sidelong glance as I wait backstage, wringing my hands together. The duet with Cole is coming up after this song, and although the run through went well earlier, it was to an empty stadium. Now, it's to a sold-out crowd of thirty thousand with a pulsing energy that's electric.

The song ends to screaming applause that takes a full minute to die down. I take a deep breath and force myself to loosen my death grip on the microphone a stagehand passed to me.

"Those of you who saw her open the show tonight were already treated to her amazing vocals, but just wait until you hear her again, on this next song. Please give a warm Atlanta welcome to none other than Macy Porter."

I step out of the shadows, into the bright lights, and make my way to Cole, who's holding a hand out for me. He does a double take, raking me from head to toe as I approach, his expression heating visibly and his bottom lip tucking between his teeth as if I'm a meal he wants to devour.

I didn't want to admit when I changed into this outfit for the duet that it was, as my Grandma Porter would say, *sending a message*, but in the recesses of my mind, I knew this look, from this man, was the goal.

And damn, if it doesn't feel good.

Cole pulls me close as the first notes of the song play. So close, the purr of approval in his throat hums against my bare shoulder and shoots south, landing in the juncture between my thighs.

I raise my mic to my lips, and it takes every ounce of focus to sing the first few bars as his warm, rough hand skims the bare skin of my lower back.

When I said the practice earlier went well, I wasn't lying, but there's something about this live performance and the heat pulsing between our bodies that skyrockets it to the next level. Our voices harmonize, and Cole holds my gaze as he sings the final chorus, as if we're alone and this is a private performance, just for me. One I'd take any day.

The deafening applause rings in my ears as I smile from ear to ear. This, right here, right now, is the moment of a lifetime. I sweep in a view of the stadium and take a deep breath, trying to absorb this sensation with every fiber of my being, so I can remember it forever.

Cole moves a few feet away and holds up an arm in my direction for me to take a bow.

"Wow, that was... That was an amazing performance by Macy Porter, ladies and gentlemen. I said you were in for a treat, and she didn't disappoint. That blew my mind. I'm... I'm speechless after that song."

I shake my head and raise an arm for him to take a bow. "Thank you, Cole, and thank you, Atlanta."

With one more wave to the crowd, I head backstage. But as I do, I catch sight of the big screen to the left of the stage and can't help but notice Cole's eyes lingering on me as I walk away.

4

Cole

Where is she?

I've been counting the minutes since Macy sashayed off stage in that short, tight skirt and those eye-catching cowboy boots, and I don't want to wait another minute to see her. To see that smile again. And more.

I scan backstage as I wipe the sweat from my brow with the back of my forearm and a sound tech grabs the mic pack from my waist.

"Great show," Ben says, weaving past the band to my side.

"Yeah." I'm exhausted, but adrenaline pumps through my veins. "Some real energy out there tonight."

I accept the bottle of water Ben offers and drain half, still searching the area with a frown.

"Do you know where—"

"She's over there."

I follow the lift of his chin to the far corner, where Macy's talking with one of the backup singers, her hands gesturing wildly as if she's recounting a story. I'm glad she's still wearing those boots because ever since she stepped onstage in those beauties with her long, lean legs on full display, I haven't been able to get an image out of my mind. An image of those boots in the air, one leg wrapped over each of my shoulders.

I start in her direction, but Ben holds me back with a hand on my arm.

"She's the real deal, Cole. I talked with her late this afternoon, and believe me, she's a sweetheart."

"Did you, by chance, find out the most important detail?"

"What's that?" Wrinkles crease his brow.

"If she's single."

Ben runs a hand through his red hair and heaves a sigh, as if admitting defeat. "I didn't ask, but I get the impression she is."

"Good."

"I had a feeling you'd say that."

"Then," I say, tossing my empty water bottle to a stagehand. "You probably also know what I'm going to do now."

5

Macy

I KNOW WHAT I'M doing—exactly what I'm getting into, but tonight, a million miles from home and from my everyday life, I don't care.

When Cole approached after the show and invited me to his bus for a drink, I said yes and knew, at that moment, exactly what I was saying yes to. But why not sleep with him? I'm a grown woman and under no delusion this is anything more than a one-night stand. But at least, it will be one night I'll remember forever.

The well-appointed, jet-black tour bus is unmarked, save for the small white Wanderlust logo on the door, a call back to Heartwood's breakthrough debut album. It sways back and forth as we turn onto the freeway, headed toward Charlotte, our next and my last stop.

Cole emerges from the back, and through the door, I spy a large bedroom that takes up the entire rear of the bus. His hair is wet from the shower, and he's barefoot, wearing ripped jeans and a black T-shirt that molds to his six-pack abs and has me convinced I made the right call.

His dark eyes flick to my legs as I sit on the long couch that runs the length of the comfy, low-lit sitting area. "Nice boots."

"Thanks." I lift my feet to admire the floral-embroidered, sand-brown, snip-toe boots. "I bought them with the first money I ever made singing."

He dips his chin toward an old, worn leather guitar case tucked against the wall. "That was my purchase. Still my favorite, besides my first guitar, but my grandpa keeps that one for me at his place in Alabama for safekeeping. He was the one who bought it for me, after all."

His eyes shine with love at the mention of his grandfather, but before I can ask anything about him, Cole opens a glass-front beverage cooler built into the bar and pulls out a bottle of beer, holding it out in my direction. "Drink? It's a," he spins the bottle to read the label, "pale ale."

I can't hide my smirk. "A favorite of yours?"

One corner of his lips tugs up, and he shrugs. "It's my one request. Wherever we tour, I have the fridge stocked with local beer, so I never know what I'm going to get. Except in your hometown, where Tessa knows to have my fridge filled with IPAs from—"

"Wait, let me guess," I say, holding up a hand. "Music City Brew Works." It's the most popular microbrewery in Nashville and a sure bet.

"Yup."

I smile. "You and every other Nashville resident."

"I don't know that I'd call myself a resident, but I've been a fan of Music City Brew since way back, before they had their brewery on Broadway. Back when they were still renting space at other breweries and trying to make a go of it. Ask Dane, he'll vouch for me."

He uses a bottle opener on the side of the counter to remove the cap from two bottles.

"You don't live in Nashville?"

He lifts a shoulder. "I've been month-to-month on a little place there for years but can count on two hands how many nights I've spent there. This," he says, waving a bottle around the bus, "is closer to home than anywhere, at least for the past few years."

He hands me a longneck and drops next to me on the couch. I take a sip and meet his eyes, sinking into the chocolate-brown irises framed by long, dark lashes but not forgetting the woman's name he mentioned a minute ago.

"And Tessa would be...?" My head tips to one side as I watch for any hint his reply might be less than truthful.

He shoots me a half-smile, and his eyebrow arches. "Not someone I've slept with."

I bite back a smile. "Do you always have to make that clarification with women you meet?"

Cole ducks his head. "Women... Hell, everyone thinks they know me because of what they've read or heard, and I just want the record straight with you."

I study him for a long minute and lift the bottle to my lips again. He may have slept with every other woman he's ever been linked to, but not, it seems, Tessa.

"I believe you."

"Good, because Tessa's my PA—and the best there is. I'd hate for her to quit because her professionalism is questioned. She's very...competent and takes her job seriously."

"Sounds like she deserves a promotion."

A low, deep chuckle emerges from his lips as he takes another swig of beer. "You're right. She probably does."

"Well, if we're being honest, I should set the record straight about something, too."

His eyes fly to mine and narrow as if he's trying to guess what I'm about to confess. "What's that?"

"Nashville's not my hometown. I've only lived there for five years."

He shifts closer on the bench, his knee brushing my thigh. "What's home for you then, if not Nashville?"

"Kissing Springs, Kentucky, romance capital of the South."

He nods. "I've heard of it and their famous strippers. You didn't find romance there?"

The miles roll by as I look toward the window, but only my eyes reflect in the glass with the dark night outside. And Cole's as he watches me. "I love Kissing Springs, but couldn't make a go of it there, you know? I had to give my dream a shot and that meant moving to Nashville."

"Based on your performance tonight, I'd say you made the right move. Plus," he says, trailing a single finger down my thigh, "I'm glad you didn't settle down. If so, you wouldn't be here with me now."

His finger stalls at my knee, the skin he's caressed on fire, and my breath catches in my throat. "No, I wouldn't."

That dangerous finger circles my knee and heads back up my thigh. Ever. So. Slowly. "You know, Macy, I've been hard since the minute you walked onstage in this skirt and those boots."

My heart pounds as loud as a bass drum when I meet his eyes, dark with desire. My tongue darts out to wet my parched lips. I've been celibate for years thanks to my single mom status and the fact Mason has always taken top priority, but tonight, my body knows exactly what it hungers for.

I run a hand up the denim of his thigh, stopping just short of the protrusion that hints at a generous cock. "Is that so?"

As fast as lightning, he snatches up my wrist and lifts it to his lips to press a kiss on the sensitive skin of my pulse point. Then he lowers it, so it's resting on his erection. "It is."

I rub up and down his length through the denim, applying pressure and relishing his sharp intake of breath. "Let's see what we can do about that, then."

Without wasting another second, he leans over and kisses me, his hand curling around the back of my neck as his lips mold to mine. And I have no regrets.

6

COLE

MACY TASTES LIKE MINT with a touch of hops, but it's the soft moan, so quiet it's almost inaudible, that emerges from her lips and sends a shiver down my spine.

She leans into me, her hand weaving through my hair, and I slide my tongue along her lower lip while I knead her thigh, slipping a finger under her skirt to caress her skin.

She scoots forward, urging me on. As if I need any encouragement.

Within seconds, she's pinned beneath me on the couch, one hand on either side of her head. Her skirt is bunched up around her hips as my knee presses against her core.

Her hips lift and grind against my thigh, seeking friction, and she looks up from under thick lashes, her chest rising and falling as her breaths come quickly.

"Cole," she murmurs, gripping my biceps.

"Yes, sweetheart." The need in her tone is like music to my ears. I trail kisses from her collarbone up to her ear. "Tell me what you want."

Her head lolls to one side, giving me greater access. "I want... I want you."

Those words have never sounded as sweet as they do falling from her lips. I want her, too, but not here. Macy deserves a bed, even if it is in the back of my tour bus.

I straighten and reach out a hand. "Come on, my bed will be more comfortable."

She slips her hand in mine, and I pull her up into my arms, unable to resist another kiss. She clutches my bicep and leans into it, her entire body pressing against me. The bus sways, and we sway along with it. I press my palm to the wall and brace us against the movement, widening my stance and tightening my hold on her.

She teases her tongue along my bottom lip. I groan and grab her hand, murmuring against her lips, "You. Are. Irresistible."

She draws back. "Lead the way."

I haul her toward the doorway as the bus hits a bump in the road, and we stumble down the narrow hallway. She giggles, and the playful sound bubbles up between us like the delicate ring of a triangle.

I kick the door closed behind us and draw her back against me. "Now, where were we?"

She grabs my hand and slides it down between us until I'm cupping her pussy.

"I think right about here." Her eyes are dark with desire, but with a touch of hesitation. *Why*? This woman is alluring in a way that goes well beyond the surface.

I trace my fingers lightly over the soft silk of her soaked panties and kiss my way to her ear. "Do you want me here?"

"Yes." Her breath catches as I increase the pressure, massaging up and down the length of her. "Please."

I shift us to the bed and climb on top of her, hitching her leg up higher at the knee. She's pinned open, and I lean back on my heels to take in the sight of her, her long, dark curls splayed out across my pillow.

Fuck, she is beautiful, and a single truth I feel in my bones like never before blazes in my mind.

One night with this woman won't be enough to satisfy my craving for her. Not even close.

I whip my shirt over my head and toss it aside. Her pupils narrow and skim down my chest to my jeans as her lip tucks between her teeth. I push away the thought of my cock between those pink lips and instead, hook a finger on either side of her panties and draw them down, licking my lips at the sight of her.

"First," I say, dropping her panties to the floor as my cock strains against the denim of my jeans, "I'm going to lick you."

I press a kiss to the smooth curve of her calf, above her boot, and settle it on my shoulder as I lower between her thighs.

"And then?" Her fingers grip the comforter, her knuckles almost white.

My mouth twitches at her curiosity, and I nip at the skin of her inner thigh, causing her to buck beneath me.

"And then," I say, taking a deep inhale of her irresistible scent. "I'm going to fuck you—hard. Does that sound good?"

Her thighs squeeze my head from either side, and her eyes screw closed. "Yes, it sounds... Yes, please."

"So polite." I swipe my tongue up the length of her warm, wet core, and my balls tighten at her sharp gasp.

It won't be hard or take long to please this woman. Within seconds of lavishing her with attention, her thighs are trembling, and her nails scrape my scalp.

Macy is uninhibited and tastes divine. I grip her hips on either side as she squirms beneath me, her moans coming louder as the bus rolls over another bump and we bounce gently.

I focus on her clit, swirling over it again and again until she tenses and moans my name. I move in, sucking and working the bud as she climaxes, a powerful orgasm rolling through her. Her boots dig into my back, pinning me to her, but there's no place on Earth I'd rather be.

When her muscles go weak and her hold eases, I draw away and meet her eyes, wiping my mouth with the back of my hand.

I probably won't last more than a minute when I fuck this beauty. My cock throbs as I relish the small, satisfied smile on her face and revel in the satisfaction thrumming through me at her pleasure.

"That was..." she says, shaking her head as if to clear the haze.

"Like a perfect harmony?"

Her lips curl into a smile. "Exactly."

"And to think, I'm not even close to done with you yet."

She lifts onto her elbows and looks around the room, her eyes landing on the built in nightstand. "You have...protection, right?"

"Yes."

"Good."

That settled, she reaches over and runs a finger along the inside waistband of my jeans. "I should hope you're not done with me then. After all, you promised to fuck me—hard."

And those words on her lips shred the last sliver of self-restraint I've been clinging to for hours.

7

Macy

I SLINK OUT TO the back curb behind the stadium and am grateful for the running town car, ready to go.

"Let me get that for you, miss." The uniformed driver reaches for my suitcase as his breath fogs like a puff of smoke in the frigid night air.

"Thank you."

I shoot one last glance at Cole's jet-black tour bus, yards away and gleaming under a pool of yellow light from a lamppost in the lot, and recall the ride I'll never forget.

Like dozens of other women before me.

Even so, the memory of the hours I spent with Cole heats my blood even now, less than twenty-four hours later.

I swallow the twinge of guilt, which tightens around my chest like an ill-fitting bra, for slipping away into the night without saying goodbye, but I need to, for my own self-preservation.

After the pleasure last night, and another lazy playful romp in bed this morning, not only am I sore in places I can't even name, but my heart is sending signals I can't succumb to. Not when Cole Heartwood is a heartbreaker, and I'm only another notch on his belt.

The roads are icy but barren as the town car, which is stifling now that I'm settled in the backseat, accelerates onto the freeway. Out the tinted window, the lights of Charlotte fly by, and I second guess myself, wondering if I should have waited until the concert finished before I left, especially after the way Cole pulled me close onstage after our duet this evening and growled in my ear, "Those boots again... You're killing me."

But the tour is rolling on, and I've got a hotel room here in Charlotte tonight and a flight home to Nashville first thing in the morning.

Another night in Cole's bed, as tempting as the thought is, is a terrible idea for a million reasons.

My phone vibrates in my lap, and I start, the sensation catching me by surprise. My pulse races until I glance at the screen and see it's not my cousin Hannah or my son's father, Hunter, both of whom are watching Mason while I'm here.

I breathe a sigh of relief and press the red X, ignoring the call from a number I don't recognize. I settle back into the seat and close my eyes, but less than a minute later, my phone buzzes again, and this time, Ben's name flashes on the screen.

I have a sinking suspicion Ben Stuart is not the man on the other end of the line.

"Hello?"

"Where the hell are you?"

I was right. And Cole's voice is deep—and furious. As if he has any right to question my whereabouts.

"I'm on my way to the hotel." I bristle.

"What?"

No, he's not furious, I realize, listening closer to his tone. He sounds almost as if he's hurt.

"I'm flying home in the morning, Cole."

There's scuffling on the other end and muffled voices. Ben, in the background, says, "Charlotte's her last stop. Why would we book a flight out of Birmingham?"

Birmingham is the tour's next stop and realization dawns on me like frostbite from a biting winter wind. Cole thought we could have another night together, and from the sound of it, it seems as if he expected it.

I try to sort out the conflicting emotions that surface with this bit of information, but before I can, Cole comes back on, his voice matter of fact. "I want to see you again."

"Why?" The question slips from my mouth before I can stop it.

"Because I... You..." He trails off, unable to articulate a reason.

"Look, Cole," I say as the town car exits the freeway. "I didn't sleep with you because I expect anything. I'm grateful for the opportunity to perform, and I enjoyed every minute. If there's another chance, I hope you or Ben think of me, but—"

"Macy," he says, cutting me off, "I want to see *you* again."

To sleep with me again he means.

I don't regret what happened, but I also don't want to spark any rumors that could damage my reputation, especially after the exposure these two nights gave me to thousands of potential new fans. I bite back a sigh. "Good luck with the rest of the tour and happy holidays."

"If you think this is goodbye, sweetheart, you're wrong."

A moment of silence stretches between us, and I swallow hard, ignoring the flutter in my belly.

"Goodnight, Cole." I hope the tremble in my voice isn't audible on the other end of the line.

I press End before I let him any further into my world, into my life that, until now, has focused solely on my son rather than on any sort of relationship with a man.

Hell, Cole doesn't even know I have a son, and that knowledge would no doubt change our perfect harmony to an offkey tune.

I stare at Mason's picture on my home screen and smile, remembering my priorities that have nothing to do with a country superstar who probably won't even remember my name next week.

NEW YEAR'S EVE | KISSING SPRINGS

I was raised on country sunshine,
green grass beneath my feet
Running through the fields of daisies,
wading through the creek
You love me and its inviting,
to go where life is more exciting
But I was raised on country sunshine
~ Country Sunshine by Dottie West

8

Cole

"The Bourbon Boot Scoot? You're sure this is the place?"

Through the SUV's tinted window, I shoot another look at the bar across the street with its weathered wooden siding and aged brick facade. A strand of multi-colored holiday lights blinks on and off around the doorway, and a bouncer, bundled up against the howling wind, kicks back on a stool with a steaming thermos in his gloved hand.

"Yes, sir. This is her location, or at least, where her phone is at the moment." Steven, my head of security, and a man not used to being questioned, informs me over his shoulder from the front seat. "She's been here less than half an hour."

The clock on the dash reads eleven-twelve p.m. Less than an hour until we ring in the New Year. Perfect timing.

Outside, a couple holding hands rushes by and crosses the empty street, sloshing through icy gray slush. They smile and wave at the bouncer, who lifts his thermos in acknowledgement, before they pass through the door into the bar.

"Security could be a little tighter, hmm?" There's no way in hell Steven will let me fly solo, but I don't mind fucking with him, just for fun.

"We'll do a sweep before you enter."

What he's really saying in that *I take no shit* tone is, he'll use bodily force to keep me from entering until he's given The Bourbon Boot Scoot the all clear.

"I'm sure that's unnecessary." I slide my phone into my coat pocket. No one, and especially not Macy Porter, who left without saying goodbye three weeks ago in Charlotte, expects me here tonight, despite the fact a video of our duet, onstage in Atlanta, has spread across the web like wildfire.

"Plus, I've got the hat," I add, picking up the stiff unworn cowboy hat at my side and running my fingers over the rigid brim.

"We'll be five minutes, tops. Wait here." Steven and my driver share a look of complete understanding before he and the other security guard, whose name I can't recall at the moment, slide out of the SUV, their eyes sweeping the quiet block in downtown Kissing Springs, Kentucky.

Five minutes is an eternity when I've come this far. I run a hand through my hair and check my watch every ten seconds as Steven and his number two talk to the bouncer, who shoots an interested glance toward the SUV.

They enter, and finally, after what feels like an eternity, a crackle breaks the dark silence and the driver lifts a finger to his earpiece.

"Alright." He meets my eyes in the rearview mirror and nods. "It's clear. Steven's got eyes on you. You're good to go."

Before he's finished speaking, I've slipped on the hat and stepped out onto the broken gravel lot, already closing the door behind me. My breath fogs in the icy air, but the cold barely registers. After all, I'm going to see Macy again, the woman I haven't been able to forget since the moment I heard her voice.

The bouncer, his mouth hanging open, holds the door for me as I slip inside. Warm, thick air blasts my face, and my eyes narrow, adjusting to the unexpected pulsing lights on a dance floor in the back.

I choke on the pungent air that smells like sweat, beer, and smoke. In an instant, it brings me back to those early days when, for months on end, we toured small-town bars just like this one and lived on hot wings and free beer.

I breathe through my mouth and survey the place. On the left, a crowded bar runs the length of the building, but Macy's not sidled up to it. Steven comes to my side and leans in, speaking loud enough to be heard over the thumping bass.

"We've secured a corner booth." He dips his chin toward the back. I acknowledge the information with a nod, but before I can respond, a glimpse of long, lean legs on the dance floor catches my attention.

Without hesitation, I move toward the figure. The long, dark curls cascading down her back confirm my sense that it's Macy, even though I can't see her face. She's wearing sky-high heels instead of those tempting boots.

I circle the dance floor, keeping to the shadows until I can see her face. An uninhibited smile, at least partly thanks to a near-empty cocktail in her hand, steals my breath.

She's even more gorgeous than I remember. Plus, her short black dress hugs her in all the right places. A twinge of doubt creeps up my spine, and I second guess my decision to surprise her on New Year's Eve in her small hometown, but she's dancing in a group, not in the arms of a man.

Without waiting another second, I step up behind her and move to the music. I couldn't have timed it better as the song shifts from a fast dance number to a slower jam.

"Can I have this dance?" I murmur, leaning in close as her friends eye me suspiciously.

Macy freezes, and a woman, about Macy's age, who's almost her spitting image and has a high flush to her cheeks, gives me a look that suggests I take a step back, *now.* She reaches for Macy as if to protect her from my unwelcome advance.

I appreciate the fact these friends have her back, but I'm not some stranger who's moving in to take advantage of a tipsy beauty who might be DTF on New Year's Eve.

Unfortunately, when Macy spins to face me, the blood drains from her face. She stumbles backward into their arms and drops her cocktail, the glass shattering into a thousand pieces across the dance floor.

9

Macy

I blink and reach up to rub my eyes at the sight before me. At the last second, I freeze, remembering in the nick of time the cat eyes slathered in glittery gold eyeshadow and rimmed by the fake lashes Chloe and Lucas insisted were perfect for our New Year's Eve night on the town. I'm certain it's not Cole Heartwood. After all, this man has a cowboy hat on, and Cole is famous for being a country music star who *never* wears a cowboy hat.

So instead, I press my hand to my chest as the dance floor clears amid screams and shouts of confusion, but I don't move. And neither does he.

I study him for a minute, but it doesn't take nearly that long to realize the tall, dark, handsome man with irresistible chocolate brown eyes staring at me is the same one who played my body like an old guitar weeks ago in Atlanta.

Two men in dark suits step up behind him, and suddenly, it's like an old-fashioned showdown on Main Street at high noon in a hot, dusty western town. Cole, with his two comrades, on one side facing off against me, with Hannah, Chloe, and Lucas drawing pistols on the other.

The situation is so surreal, and the image in my mind so hilarious, an uncontrollable giggle bubbles up from my chest.

Cole does not look amused. His jaw clenches, and he steps toward me as a server approaches. Her boots crunch on the shattered glass, and she's got a wide broom in hand.

"Macy," Cole says, reaching for me. "Careful of the glass in those heels."

Even as drunk as I am, I can tell he's speaking slowly, as if to a child, and I giggle even more at the absurd realization.

"Do you know this guy?" Hannah asks, confusion knotting her brow.

"Yes." I pull myself together with a deep breath and, gripping her arm, back carefully off the dance floor, the music still blaring from the speakers. "It's Cole."

Cole, who doesn't look as if he's about to leave my side, moves with us. "Cole, Hannah. Hannah, Cole." I shoot her a wink, impressed I remembered my manners, and introduced them properly.

Hannah's head tilts to the side, and it takes a second, but realization dawns and her eyes widen. "Cole Heartwood Cole?"

"OMG," Lucas exclaims, his jaw dropping. "It is. It's Cole Heartwood, right here in the Bourbon Boot Scoot!"

"Macy, I—" Cole begins before Chloe interrupts, her grip tight on my arm.

"Do you want me to call Tony?"

"No," I assure her, my foggy brain clearing quickly as the reality of the situation hits and my stomach lurches. "I don't need security. I think I just need to sit down."

In less than a second, Cole has his arm around my shoulders, supporting my full weight, and is leading me to an empty booth in the corner.

"Water. Now." He speaks over his shoulder in a low voice so commanding I nearly spin to follow the order.

"Not you," he says, his grip tightening around me.

I can't help it. I lean into his solid frame and enjoy the sizzle of desire at his proximity. Proximity I've fantasized about a handful of times in the past few weeks.

Okay, maybe, more than a handful.

My dress rides up my thigh as I slide onto the worn wooden bench, and Cole spins to face my entourage. But before he can speak, Hannah pipes up, holding out a hand on either side of her body to stall Chloe and Lucas.

"Let's give them some space, okay?"

I give them a thumbs up and a smile, and they reluctantly move away a few feet, although Chloe still shoots furtive glances over her shoulder at us as Lucas pulls out his phone.

Cole slides in next to me until his thigh is pressed against mine, tethering me to an unimaginable reality.

I turn to face him. "Are you here for me?"

He removes his hat and meets my eyes, and it might be my imagination, but his expression seems to soften. "Yes."

"Why?"

He cocks an eyebrow. "How many drinks have you had?"

I'm drunk enough to know there's no way I could give him an accurate number. Between the pre-partying at Hannah's, the featured holiday cocktails at the Hot Derby Nights, and however many more I've had since we arrived at the bar, I'm toast.

"You look...different in a cowboy hat."

"Well, don't get used to it. I hate 'em."

I'm confounded by the vehemence in his tone, but before I can ask about it, he repeats his question.

"How many drinks have you had, Macy?"

My nose wrinkles. "A lot."

"That's what I thought."

"How many drinks have you had?" I ask. I might have just slurred the question, but I lean in, and his gaze slips from my face to the crevice at the low-cut neckline of my dress. But, before he can answer, one of his men returns with a large glass of iced water and a straw. Cole drags his gaze back up and acknowledges the delivery with a nod.

His two men both wear earpieces and flank the booth, watching the crowd, half of whom couldn't seem to care less, while the other half can't seem to contain their excitement.

"Are they bodyguards?" I whisper, leaning in close and nodding toward the men.

Cole unwraps the straw and sticks it in the glass, sliding it toward me. "Drink this."

When he shifts, the scent of his cologne fills the air. And suddenly, it's like I'm back on the tour bus. Alone. With him.

"You smell nice, just like last time."

He freezes, and a smile tugs at his lips. "Drink some water."

It's not a command this time as he lifts the glass, but a plea. I accept the pint glass and draw the straw between my lips, noting the way his eyes are glued to them.

After a long sip, watching him through lowered lashes and feeling sexy and bold as hell, I set down the glass and realize Cole doesn't have a drink.

"Excuse me, sir."

The suited man standing guard next to our booth turns to me, his gaze flicking to Cole.

"Yes, ma'am?"

Ma'am?

"Um, yes. Could you please get Cole a Music City Pale Ale?"

Cole answers the man's questioning glance with a barely perceptible nod, and the man moves off, circling the dance floor that's filled up again now that the broken glass has been cleared.

I'm glad to see Chloe, Hannah, and Lucas back out there, but an unsettled thought I can't quite put my finger on nags at the back of my mind.

Before I can wade through the haze and pick it out of the murky recesses, Cole lays a warm, heavy hand on my thigh. The sensation shoots through me, and my breath catches.

I feel as if I'm moving in slow motion, my thoughts not keeping pace with my body, but before I can stop myself, I blurt out, "Are you here to fuck me?"

10

Cole

"DO YOU WANT ME to fuck you?"

"Yes." Macy's answer is definitive and almost instant.

My cock hardens at the single word until she adds, "But I can't."

She's not playing hard to get or toying with me. No, she's dead serious, despite her inebriated state.

"Why not?" I'm genuinely perplexed. Still, I'm hopeful her answer will provide insight on whatever the issue is here that didn't exist three weeks ago in Atlanta and if it's something I can potentially overcome.

I came here for Macy, and I'd be lying if I said sleeping with her didn't cross my mind, but more than that, I wanted to see her again, to hear her voice and figure out why, weeks later, I still can't get her out of my head.

Unlike every other woman who's come before her.

Her curls swing from side to side as she shakes her head. "It's against my policy."

I lean back. "Tell me more."

"I have a—thank you," she says to Steven, who returns with the requested bottle and sets it on the table.

"Cheers." I lift the bottle and take a long drink, aware of her eyes on me the entire time, watching my mouth and not trying to hide the fact she's mesmerized. Hell, she probably doesn't realize she's staring.

It's a good sign. She might be through with me, might want nothing to do with me, but she's still attracted to me.

That used to be enough. But with Macy, I have an odd sense there's something more than simply attraction between us, even though the video posted online after Atlanta proves we have chemistry in spades.

"You have a what?" I prompt after I set down the beer and she doesn't continue.

"What?"

"You were explaining why you can't sleep with me tonight."

"I told you. I have a policy."

From the corner of my eye, I see Steven shift on his feet and shoot a look at his number two, dipping his chin toward the dance floor. My gaze follows, and Macy's sister, or at least a blood relation of some sort, has her arms wrapped around a man who's just arrived and is studying Macy and me cuddled up here in the corner booth. Whatever she tells him, he seems to accept, and he turns his attention back to the woman with a smile.

And I turn my attention back to Macy, who's oblivious to the interchange. I slip my arm around her shoulder and pull her closer.

"But what is the policy, sweetheart?"

"Sweetheart, hmm?" The corner of her lips curls into a half smile. "You don't strike me as the romantic type Cole Heartwood."

Drunk Macy is proving to be very forthcoming, and I love this uncensored view into her thoughts. "No? What do I strike you as, then?"

Her lips purse, as if considering the question, and her thumb absently runs up and down the side of her glass. "More like a love 'em and leave 'em type."

"If I recall correctly, you're the one who left without saying goodbye."

She has the grace to look guilty. "I...I thought you'd gotten what you wanted, and I did, too."

"An orgasm?"

"Yup. A great one, too. Hell, wasn't it three or even four, come to think of it?"

Yes, sweetheart, yes, it was. "And you don't want another one tonight?"

She slides a hand over my thigh to press against the length of my erection under the zipper of my jeans. "Oh, I do, believe me. But I can't. I have a policy."

I grit my teeth. She's not trying to tease me; rather, she's being so matter of fact I wonder if the water isn't doing some good to bring her blood alcohol level down. "You said that, sweetheart, but what is the policy?"

"That I don't sleep with men when I'm drunk."

Not what I expected, but I can't help but respect it. "That's a good policy."

"So you see," she says, leaning in and, thankfully, drawing her hand off my cock to walk her fingers up my chest. "That's why I can't fuck you tonight."

I do see.

"But..." she says, squinting as if she's trying to work out something in her mind. "I suppose that doesn't rule out doing *other* things."

Perfect.

"What kind of *other* things?" I whisper in her ear as my thumb caresses her bare shoulder.

It takes a second, and I'm captivated by the thoughts flickering through her eyes until she realizes what I'm asking and her breath hitches.

She swallows, and her tongue darts out to skim her lips. She hesitates for the briefest instant before saying, "You could lick me."

And I thought I was already hard as a rock. My jaw clenches, and my grip on the bottle tightens until my knuckles are pure white.

I meet her eyes. "I'd love to lick your pussy again, Macy, and make you come. Could I use my fingers, too? I want to hear those moans of pleasure I so enjoyed last time."

"Yes," she murmurs, breathless, as her hand slides under the table and caresses my erection again. "But only if I get to blow you."

"Deal," I growl, grabbing her hand and sliding to the edge of the booth.

She giggles, but her fingers tighten around mine, and she follows, drawing up next to me and wobbling on her feet as she grabs my belt for balance.

"Alright there?" I weave an arm around her waist.

"Yes, but we can't leave yet. It's almost New Year's."

She's right. A quick glance at my phone confirms it's five 'til twelve. "How about a dance?"

Her face lights up like fireworks, and she practically drags me toward the dance floor, her hips already swaying to the beat and an arm in the air.

We join the throng and disappear into the holiday crowd. I don't give Steven, and the fact he's probably cursing me right about now, another thought, because I can't. Macy, in her tight black dress and fuck-me high heels, press against my body, and she deserves every bit of my attention.

After another song, the DJ breaks in and starts a countdown, but before we hit midnight, Macy's lips are pressed against mine, and her arms are wrapped around my neck.

I grip her hips, my fingers digging into her flesh, as she wriggles against me. Her tongue skates along my lips, teasing and probing, and I can't resist another second. I crush her to me, weaving my hand through her hair and holding her head to mine as I delve into her mouth, fusing her to me.

A moan escapes her, and we're oblivious to the merriment around us as the crowd cheers in the new year.

It is, by far, the most memorable New Year's Eve kiss I've had in my life. Hell, it's the hottest kiss I've ever had, and that's saying a lot.

"Fuck, Macy," I swear, tearing away and dragging in a lungful of air. "Let's go."

"So you can lick me," she whispers in my ear as she falls against me.

"Yes, sweetheart." I assure her this is the case, although by now I know it's not in the cards tonight. She needs sleep, more water, and probably some aspirin.

"Happy New Year, Macy," I murmur, enveloping her in my arms and resting my chin on her head as the rest of the bar, the rest of the world, falls away.

"Happy New Year, Cole," she says, snuggling against me.

11

Macy

I ROLL OVER AND bury my head under a pillow, squeezing my eyes shut against the blinding sunlight streaming in through the window. I'd give anything to fall back asleep, but the ache pounding in my head, like a jackhammer on concrete, is relentless.

I tug the covers up over my head. It helps enough that I drift off, but just when I start to succumb to slumber, the hair on the back of my neck rises. There's a shifting of limbs next to me. And not my son's tiny arms and legs. No, this movement is enough to shake the mattress and make the old headboard in the guest room at what I still think of as Grandma Porter's house creak.

I gasp and then hold my breath as my mind whirls, trying to put together the fragmented memories from last night, piece by piece, like a toy train that snaps together from engine to caboose.

I nearly squeak but catch myself at the last second and keep my mouth closed tight, still cocooned under the old quilt and now afraid to move a muscle. It's Cole. Cole Heartwood is here, in the guest bed with me at Hannah's house in Kissing Springs.

At least, I hope it's Cole.

I'm going to throw up.

I swallow hard and try not to think about the bitter taste in the back of my throat as saliva floods my mouth.

As slow as a sloth, I peek out from under the covers and spot Cole, bare chested, with one arm flung up over his head, sleeping like a baby.

The relief that it's not a random guy I don't know lasts about a millisecond before I curse my past self.

Shit. Shit. Shit.

We didn't sleep together last night. At least, I don't think we did. The last thing I remember is dancing at the Bourbon Boot Scoot just as midnight rolled around. And after that... I got nothin.

I bite my lip, debating what to do, when the front door bangs open downstairs, and Hunter greets my son, Mason, with a loud, "Happy New Year, buddy!"

My face scrunches up because I'm a thousand percent sure Cole's about to wake up, and that would be more awkward than forgetting the lyrics onstage mid-song.

When he rolls over and mumbles something in his sleep, stretching out an arm in my direction, I take advantage of the movement to slide out of bed, my bare feet silently hitting the cold wood floor.

It works. He settles in as I shiver, a chill running up my spine despite the red-and-black plaid flannel pajamas I have on.

Pajamas I don't remember putting on.

My hands fly to my breasts.

No bra.

Not bothering with slippers, I back out of the room, praying the creaky door doesn't alert him to my covert escape.

It's not until I hit the bottom step of the stairs that I notice my racing heartbeat. I take a deep breath and will it to return to normal. Or as normal as it can be given the circumstances.

Mason tears through the hallway with Daisy, Hunter's dalmatian, hot on his heels.

"Mommy!"

He tumbles into my arms, and I give him a tight squeeze, despite the pounding in my head. Before I can speak, I have to clear my throat and lick my dry, cracked lips. "Did you have fun last night with Uncle Tanner, honey?"

He pulls away and recounts his entire evening at warp speed, which is impossible to follow thanks to my hangover and still thumping head.

"Coffee?" Hannah, my cousin, holds out a steaming Christmas mug in my direction.

"Please."

The brew smells like heaven, and I clasp it in both hands as she glances up the stairs before she meets my eyes.

"Hey, Mason, I think your dad is outside with Uncle Tanner. Why don't you take Daisy out there and play catch?"

"Okay." He spins and clambers out through the back door, Daisy right behind him, as I take a scalding sip of coffee.

"You have a visitor," Hannah says, as if making a casual observation about a new way I styled my hair instead of the fact a famous singer is asleep upstairs in my bed.

The back door slams, and I wince at the sound—and the reverberations going through my cranium. "I know. Don't ask."

"Not Cole." She crooks a finger, beckoning me toward the front window, and draws back the faded cotton curtain. A black SUV with dark tint is parked across the street and two houses down. With a man in the driver's seat.

"I'm sure Mrs. McArthur is all over this," she adds as I swallow and try not to surrender to the panic rising inside me.

This is all too much. One thought overpowers every other one whirling through my mind. I've got to get out of here with Mason before Cole wakes up.

"I've got to go. Now. Can you help get Mason's stuff together while I get dressed?"

Her forehead wrinkles. "Where are you going?"

"Home." I shove the hot mug back into her hands and spin around, frantic.

"Macy!"

"What?" I whisper-shout, shooting a look back upstairs.

"You can't leave him here!" She jerks a finger toward my room.

"Why not? He's still sleeping. Plus, when he wakes up, he's already got a ride."

"But—"

"Look," I say, grabbing her arm. "I don't want Mason to see a half-naked, strange man waking up in my bed and—"

I freeze and trail off, considering the opposite. What would Cole say if he saw my son, a child he doesn't even know exists?

It's not as if it matters. There's nothing between Cole and me, despite the internet rumors that flew after that video of us was posted online. I'm just a booty call gone wrong.

But even as the thought crosses my mind, there's a whiff of something not quite right about it.

I don't remember everything that happened last night, but from what I can piece together, Cole was a perfect gentleman. Which I didn't expect. Not that it matters right now.

"Please help me get out of here." I press my hands together in front of my chest. "Please, Hannah."

"And what am I supposed to tell Cole when he wakes up and you're gone?"

"Tell him I had to go and that next time, he should call before he just shows up—no, on second thought, don't say that. Just tell him—"

She shoos me off. "I'll figure something out. Now go, I'll get Mason's stuff and meet you out front."

I give her a brief side hug and a half smile. "Thanks for a great time last night. Really."

"It was a fun night on the town, wasn't it? And hey, you didn't seem upset when Cole walked into the bar. In fact, you fell right into his arms."

I can't help it. "Could be worse arms to fall into, hmm?"

"Could be," she agrees, giving me a knowing smile I return.

12

Cole

I CAN SLEEP ANYWHERE. It's one of the many things I learned out of necessity my first few years on the road and a skill I've used ever since.

But tucked in bed last night, with Macy curled against my side, I didn't even have to try. I fell asleep faster than a tired baby listening to a lullaby. And slept like a log.

But now, as I wake up, memories from last night fill my mind. Especially the drunk, drowsy, sexy quips Macy bantered with me on the way out to the SUV. But, just as I figured she would, the irresistible woman passed out within seconds of settling in the backseat.

At least, she gave Steven the address to drop us off first. Her cousin's house here in Kissing Springs used to belong to their grandmother.

Then she kicked off her heels, tucked up her legs, rested her head on my shoulder, and was out like a light. I shifted her so my thigh was her pillow and spent the short ride watching the peaceful expression on her gorgeous face and wondering what would happen in the morning.

I'm glad I came to see her. More than glad if I'm being honest. Macy was exactly as I remembered and then some. She's everything I haven't been able to forget since she appeared in my life last month and staked a claim without even knowing it.

Once we got here, I spotted the flannel pajamas folded on the chair in the corner. I hoped she wouldn't mind me helping her into them. It wasn't easy, but with some patient maneuvering, I slipped off her dress and wrangled them on her nearly naked body, trying my best to ignore the memory of worshiping her with my hands and tongue and body weeks ago.

Just thinking about how she fell apart in my tour bus last month makes my morning wood twitch now, so I stretch and reach for her. My mind clears instantly, snapping to the present—an inconceivable present—when I find only cool sheets instead of her soft, warm body.

I lift up on my elbows and glance around the empty room. My stomach drops, but before I jump to conclusions, I pick up on the hum of conversation and people moving around downstairs. Macy must be down there with them.

Eager to see her and see how she's feeling this morning, I throw on my shirt and jeans and make my way down the creaky stairs to the kitchen.

But she's nowhere in sight.

Hunter, the man I met last night on our way out of the bar, pours coffee at the counter. Hannah, Macy's cousin, sits at the table with another man who's got to be related to Hunter somehow, what with their nearly identical dark coloring.

But Macy's not here.

A dalmatian noses under my hand, and I absently scratch behind her ears, while my brow furrows.

"Macy had to go, but she said to say goodbye."

I meet Hannah's eyes across the table, confusion rocketing through me. This is not a scenario I would have dreamed of in a hundred years.

"Go where?"

"Home."

No. No way she gave me the slip again. "To Nashville?"

Hannah's expression falters at my question as if she feels my surprise...and my disappointment.

"Yes, but," she rushes to add, "she's glad you came to surprise her. She said it was nice to see you."

There's no way I can follow Macy now, no matter how much I'd like to track her down and kiss her senseless. Kiss her and then use my other talents to convince her to tell me why she keeps slipping through my fingers. I have to be in Louisville by two for the show tonight.

My hands curl into fists at my side. "If it was so *nice* to see me, why did she slip away again without saying goodbye?"

Hannah and Hunter exchange a look as he slides onto the chair next to her at the table and then jerks his head toward the coffeemaker.

"Coffee, Cole? Help yourself."

"Yes, of course. Where are my manners?" Hannah exclaims, jumping up and waving me in from the doorway. "And Happy New Year, too."

"Happy New Year," I mutter, accepting the mug she pushes toward me. "Thanks."

Hannah rests a hand on my arm and meets my eyes. She's wearing glasses, but underneath, her eyes are the same shade of baby blue as Macy's. The similarity knots my stomach.

"She said, maybe, to call first next time, before you just show up." Hannah forces out the words, almost apologetically, as if she wishes she weren't the one passing on the request.

"Is that so?"

"Yes," she squeaks and slinks back to her chair.

I pour a cup of coffee and join them at the table, the bracing sip of hot black brew not helping my foul mood.

"Well, since we're passing along messages and you seem to be the go-between, would you mind telling Macy I want to see her again?"

"Are you going to follow her to Nashville?" Hunter's voice is low, and he doesn't meet my eyes. There's a touch more than curiosity in his voice. Something I can't quite put my finger on but isn't exactly friendly.

I shake my head. "I can't. I need to be in Louisville this afternoon. We've got six more weeks until this tour wraps."

He nods but says nothing more.

"Hey, man, are you...?" The other man, his forehead wrinkling, shoots a questioning look at Hunter before his eyes swing back to me.

"Cole Heartwood, nice to meet you." I swallow my anger for a moment and extend a hand. After all, these people all know Macy and may be close to her. Close enough to convince her to see me again.

"Tanner Williams," the man says slowly as he shakes my outstretched hand, his head falling to the side. "I'm Hunter's brother. But...weren't you on TV last night? On that New Year's Eve special from New York?"

That explains his confusion.

"I was, but we taped that performance weeks ago."

"Oh."

"Last night, we performed in Knoxville" I glance toward Hannah. "That's the only reason I made it here to Kissing Springs to surprise Macy. We sped here at a hundred miles an hour."

She jerks her head toward the street outside. "Your ride is still out front."

I'm not surprised. Steven probably spent the entire night out there, dozing in the SUV. If he did, he must have seen Macy leaving this morning and may have more details about what happened.

"Good, thanks."

I push back in my chair and rise, but step on something under the table. I reach down and retrieve a Hot Wheels fire truck, just like one I had when I was young.

I set it on the table, and Tanner reaches for it, picking it up and turning it over in his hand. "This is the one Mason was looking for last night. He wanted to show it to me during the sleepover but couldn't find it."

"Mason?" I ask, looking around for a little boy who's nowhere to be seen.

Hannah's expression shifts to one of panic, and I'm not sure why until she blurts out, "Yeah, Mason, Hunter's son."

At the same time, Tanner says, "Yeah, Mason, Macy's son."

What the hell?

Valentine's Day | Nashville

I was raised on country sunshine,
I'm happy with the simple things
A Saturday night dance, a picture show and the joy that a bluebird brings
I love you please believe me,
I won't want you to ever leave me
But I was raised on country sunshine
~ Country Sunshine by Dottie West

13

MACY

MY FINGERS SETTLE AT C position on the smooth keys of my old piano. I clear my throat and look over the song lyrics in my notebook. The lyrics resemble chicken scratches since I've scribbled them out and rewritten different versions a million times over the past month.

"I wish I could forget, put you out of my mind, but every time I close my eyes, you're the one I find," I murmur, listening to see if changing the chord helps. It doesn't.

I sing the chorus then heave a sigh, sinking back on the bench, and flick a glance at my phone on the wide windowsill on my right.

I reach for it then stop myself. Checking social media or my email right now will not get me any closer to finishing this song. Although I have a dozen half-baked ideas jotted down, I haven't gotten far on a single one since last year. And now, it's almost Valentine's Day.

Checking on my son won't get me any closer, either, but Mason's been quiet for way too long. Which means he's probably up to no good.

Sure enough, a trail of red glitter down the hallway leads to his room. Just as I reach the doorway, he pops up from the floor and holds up both hands, trying to block me from entering.

"Whatcha doing?" I ask, peering over and around him.

"Nothin'." He does his best *I'm as innocent as an angel* face. The one I've never been able to resist.

I smile and kneel. "That's little boy code for something. Plus," I say, swiping a few pieces of glitter from the floor on my fingertip, "it looks like *nothing* is messy."

"I'm using tape, Mommy, not glue. I promise."

There's a smudge of red marker across his cheek, and I bite back a smile. "Any chance this secret project is for school tomorrow?"

I've volunteered to help with the preschool class Valentine's Day party, and Mason's been talking nonstop about it all week.

He shakes his head. "I finished my Valentines for school last night."

"Of course. How could I forget? Those were the best dinosaur Valentines I've ever seen."

"And the box, too," he adds, reminding me of the tissue box he decorated to look like a Tyrannosaurus Rex.

"Sounds like you're all set for tomorrow."

"So you can go back to playing," he says, his small hands pressing me back, away from the door.

"You sure?" I try to catch another glimpse of his room, but he starts to close the door.

"Yup."

"Okay, but dinner is in an hour." I ruffle his hair as I rise and head back down the hall. "And be sure to clean up whatever you've got going on in there for Mommy, alright?"

"Okay," he promises as the door clicks closed. I make a mental note to check on him in ten minutes.

I settle back at the piano and catch a notification light up on my phone. Hannah, my cousin, has sent a link. Only the first few words are visible, but it doesn't matter. I saw the article in the online version of *The Country Music Chronicle* this morning and read the profile on Cole Heartwood, country royalty and notorious playboy, word-for-word. Twice.

Determined not to let thoughts of *him* distract me any more today, I turn my attention back to the song, but the phone vibrates on the windowsill.

"Hey," I say, answering Hannah's call with speakerphone. It's not as if I was getting anywhere, anyway.

"Did you see what I just sent you?"

What? No hello?

"I read it this morning."

"Oh."

Damn. Her perceptive tone tells me, if we were playing poker right now, I just showed my hand.

"And...?" she asks, trailing off and waiting for me to elaborate.

I press my lips together. What can I say? Hannah has encouraged me to call Cole a hundred times since I left him high and dry on New Year's Day. And I haven't.

Plus, I'd better not mention the screenshot I took this morning of the picture posted with the article. The one I saved in my photos. As a favorite.

"You know I'm not about to ride his coattails. I've told you before, Cole was a one-night stand, nothing more."

"Macy, that video of you two is still making the rounds online months later, and the man tracked you down on New Year's Eve and drove almost two hundred miles to see you."

As if I need to be reminded.

I ignore the curl of warmth in my belly at the hazy memory of that night and shake my head.

"I have a son I need to think about, you know."

"Lots of single parents date. It's not like you'd be the first."

"They don't date country music's biggest star."

"But you are still interested in him."

It's not a question, and damn, there's that tone again.

"I didn't say that."

"But you don't deny it."

She knows me too well.

My phone lights up with another incoming call.

"Hold on a second," I say, pausing the conversation that's going nowhere fast. "Actually, can I call you back? It's my agent on the other line."

"Sure, yeah. Plus, I want to talk about this weekend, too."

"Mason's really looking forward to your visit. But yeah, I'll talk to you later. Bye."

I press the button on my phone screen to switch calls and rise, popping in my earbuds. I pace around the family room, now too agitated at the mention of Cole to sit still.

"Hello?"

"Macy, you are not going to believe this."

I can't count the number of times I've heard this exact phrase from my overly enthusiastic agent since I signed with her four years ago, but I play along, as I always do.

"What?"

"Really, this is big. Are you sitting down?"

I sink onto the couch, so I don't have to lie. "I'm sitting down."

"Okay." She takes a deep breath and pauses for dramatic effect as I rise and continue the laps around my way-too-small family room. "You know that video of the duet you did with Cole Heartwood onstage in Atlanta?"

Why is everyone still talking about that video?

"Yes." I draw out the word as my mind spins with potential scenarios of why she's bringing this up now—none of them good.

"It's. Gone. Viral. And not just a little viral. A lot viral. As in something like sixty-one million views and counting."

"*Sooo…*" I say, trying my best to ignore the knot in my stomach.

"*Sooo*... I just got off the phone with Ben Stuart—you know, Cole's manager—and they want you to come in and record the song, so it can be released as a single!"

My jaw drops, and I press a palm to my belly, the knot morphing to a lurching lump. "What? Really?"

"Yup. Can you believe it? You're going to have a chart-topping song!"

"Who's *they* exactly?"

"What?"

"You said *they* want me to come in to record it. It is just the label or..."

"I'm not sure," she says, confusion slowing her answer. "I think he mentioned something about Cole, but I don't remember exactly."

I wave a hand even though she can't see it. "Forget I asked. It doesn't matter. Of course, I'm happy to go into the studio and record the song with him. When are they looking to do it?"

I click on the calendar app on my phone but freeze when she says, "Tomorrow."

"*Tomorrow* tomorrow?"

"I know it's short notice, but I assured Ben it wouldn't be a problem."

It might be a problem. "What time? I've got Mason's class party from one to two-thirty."

"Noon."

I consider my options for less than a minute. "I'm sorry. I can't be there until three."

"What? Macy—"

I cut her off. "If it's a deal breaker that I'm not there at noon, let me know tonight. Otherwise, I'll see them at three."

“Okay...” she says, sounding as if she fully expects to call me back. But then adds, “Are you excited? You sound... I don’t know, like maybe, you’re nervous, which is totally normal.”

If only she knew Cole Heartwood and I slept together the day that viral video was recorded. The day we met. And then, weeks later, on New Year’s Eve, how he surprised me at the bar in my hometown just before midnight.

“I’m excited, I swear.”

We hang up, and I pull out my earbuds and toss the phone back on the windowsill. I stare at it, my heartbeat pounding at the thought I’ll see Cole again in less than twenty-four hours.

Then, before I can help myself, I snatch the phone back up and click on the photos app, zooming in on the last image.

Cole Heartwood, with his dark eyes and famous drop-dead gorgeous smile, stares back at me, and a fissure of heat pools in my core.

14

Cole

I SHOULD BE IN the booth using these reserved hours to actually record or at least mess around with the band to see what we come up with, but instead, I'm pacing back and forth, my blood pressure rising with every car that pulls into the lot that isn't a ruby red Mustang.

That's what Macy drives, and thanks to the Tennessee plate Steven, my bodyguard, snapped a picture of in Kissing Springs on New Year's Day—and some low-key detective work he accomplished in a matter of minutes—I've had her car registration information and address for six weeks now.

It's been burning a hole in my pocket. Sure, I've been busy on tour, but also, I've been biding my time, waiting for today, to record with her amazing vocals, but more importantly, just to see her again.

Finally, at five 'til three, she pulls in. I freeze, my fingers gripping the windowsill, and watch from my spot on the second floor. It's a long minute before her driver's door swings open, but when it does and first one leg then the second emerges and both hit the ground, I shake my head and rub my hand over my cheeks. And my smile.

Things aren't over between us, not by a long shot. In fact, one might even say they're just beginning. After all, she wore *those* boots. The brown embroidered ones that stole my attention that first night onstage in Atlanta when she filled in as the opener on our tour and sang with me. The same ones I admired later that night on my tour bus and that she wore when I wrapped her legs over my shoulders and made her come.

"There you are." Ben's red head peeks in the doorway, interrupting my thoughts. "Steven said I could find you here."

I'm not surprised. Steven keeps closer tabs on me than a mother on her newborn.

"No, I was just..."

"Watching for Macy?"

I don't answer.

He steps into the conference room and clasps the back of the chair at the end of the table with both hands. "You've been waiting for today for a while, I know. But, as I said yesterday, if she said she'd be here at three, she'll be here. We both know she's not the type to not show."

"No, she's not."

But she is one to slip away without saying goodbye. At least, last time, on New Year's Day, she had a good reason, or a reason I can forgive her for, anyway, even if I didn't like it at the time.

"You're looking forward to seeing her again."

His observation is spot on, and I can't help but nod. "I am."

"There must really be something there. Something between you two for you to go to all this trouble."

I run a hand through my hair and shoot one more look out the window, but she's disappeared inside the building. Convincing the label to release a single wasn't hard. They know as well as I do anything Macy Porter and I collaborate on at the moment will top the charts.

As much as I trust Ben, I'm not about to admit that, after the blistering night in December, and especially after the surprising

New Year's Eve, I can't get Macy Porter out of my head. Especially because I'm finding it hard to believe I don't want to forget her. Not even a little. I want to see her again and see where this goes. Hell, maybe, give a relationship a real chance for the first time ever.

"Well," I say, clapping Ben on the back while he eyes me suspiciously before I make my way out of the room. "There's only one way to find out."

MACY STEPS OFF THE elevator in a red knit sweater and tight black pants, looking like a million dollars, and meets my eyes.

"You look amazing."

Her lips press together as if to hide a small smile. "You're not too shabby yourself."

"Thanks. It's good to see you." I step forward, drawn to her. I want to pull her against me and wrap my arms around her again, just like on the dance floor at The Bourbon Boot Scoot on New Year's Eve, but she stiffens, and I catch myself.

Give her a minute, Cole. She only found out about today's recording session yesterday, not a month ago, when I started planning it.

"It's good to see you, too." Her voice is low but sincere, and her words confirm my instinct that today things between us will change, evolve, exactly as I'd hoped.

"Ready to sing?"

She meets my eyes. "I'm ready."

Good.

"This way then." I head down the hallway, and she quickly falls in step at my side.

There's so much I want to say, but there'll be time enough for that later. For now, I want to put her at ease and enjoy recording with her.

From the corner of my eye, I glimpse something white in her hair. I pull up short, and she stops, too. I reach for whatever it is. "You have something in your hair."

She looks down and holds out the section of dark curls in one hand and digs in her purse for a tissue with the other. Then, she tries to extract the glob, although the squishy consistency makes it next to impossible.

She laughs and keeps wiping. "It's frosting."

"Frosting?"

"That's why I'm late. I volunteered this afternoon at my..." She falters for a second, barely enough to catch, but I notice. And I respect the way she lifts her chin before she finishes. "At my son's Valentine's Day party in his classroom at school—well, preschool, but we call it school."

"Mason's five, right?"

Wide sky-blue eyes meet mine, and Macy hesitates as a young woman approaches from down the hallway, giving us a wide berth as she passes, but then answers. "Yes."

"Was it fun?"

"What?"

"The Valentine's Day party. Did you have fun?"

Her face lights up, and her lips curl into a smile as she lifts the lock of hair as evidence. "We had a blast."

"Good. I'm glad you were there."

"Me, too. Thanks for accommodating my schedule. I know how expensive studio time is."

I wave off her gratitude. "You chose the more important thing. Believe me, I should know."

"What do you mean?"

We resume our walk down the hallway, and I give her a sidelong glance, my chest tightening at the memories of searching for a glimpse of my mom in the stands or on the sideline. "I'm an only child raised by a single mom. I would have given anything for her to have been able to come to my activities, but she never could. She was always busy working two jobs to support us."

She's quiet for a minute. "You were lucky to have her."

"I know that now, but back then, it stung."

She lays a hand gently on my forearm. "You were just a little boy."

I'm grateful my mom always scraped together enough to pay the fees for t-ball or soccer or whatever it was, but I'm not sure I want to know exactly how she came up with the extra money. I was thrilled to participate, but she was never in the stands to see me play, never on the sidelines for my good days or bad. Sure, I filled her in later, but it was never the same.

I sigh and shake off the memories, grateful for my success because it means she'll never have to work another day in her life. I glance down at Macy's hand resting on my arm. "I'm just saying I'm glad you went, even when this came up at the last minute."

I don't want Macy to know today's session has been in the works for weeks. Don't want her to discover the reason I didn't have Ben call her manager the second the studio was booked was because I was worried if she had too much time to consider the opportunity, she'd come up with a reason not to record with me, no matter how much this single could help her career.

"Cole," she says, squeezing my arm to hold me back before we turn into the sound room attached to the booth. She lowers her voice and meets my eyes. "I'm sorry for ghosting you on New Year's morning. I—"

I can't help it. I pull up short and pin her, my palm pressed flat against the wall on one side of her face while I leave an out in case she wants to slip away. But she doesn't. She meets my eyes and opens her mouth to continue, but I lean in, and the words stall on her lips.

"Macy," I murmur, trying to keep the need from my tone. "May I kiss you?"

Her tongue darts out to wet her lips, and she tugs the bottom one between her teeth before she nods.

It's enough. I erase the inches between us and clasp her waist with my free hand, melting into a kiss I've craved for weeks.

It takes barely a second before Macy's tension releases and she leans in with a soft moan, meeting me in the middle. And just like that, the fire is back, crackling between us. An electricity that started during that first sound check and nearly combusted later that night onstage.

I wrench away and drag in a lungful of air.

Macy's chest heaves, and her eyes are wide as she glances up and down the empty hallway. "Cole—"

I cut her off with one last quick kiss and murmur, "I've wanted to do that ever since I rolled over in bed on New Year's Day and you were gone. Have wanted to do it every day since."

"Really?"

The question is tinged with honest surprise, and her eyes narrow on me with suspicion. And I don't blame her one bit.

"Really. Now, let's go record a song."

15

Macy

"What do you think about riffing this section, kind of like how you do in *Hearts on Fire?*"

Cole points to a bar on the sheet music with the tip of a No. 2 pencil, but I'm too distracted to focus on it. This is the fourth time in the past two hours he's referenced a song in my catalog. And not just the songs, but very specific sections within them, as we've been recording and re-recording, making adjustments to the harmony and the vocals.

I've only released two albums, so my catalog isn't extensive, but still. I don't have to wonder anymore what he's been doing for the last few weeks—besides touring, of course.

But the knowledge of how he's spent the time away, when I thought he'd moved on, has raised another question in my mind. One I'm trying not to dwell on at the moment, which is really, really hard.

What now?

Where do things go from here? Cole and I met in December and slept together that first night. I thought that would be the end of it. I mean, he's a famous country heartthrob with a larger-than-life reputation as a ladies' man. But then, he showed up on New Year's Eve, surprised me at the bar in Kissing Springs, spent the night taking care of my drunk ass...and not sleeping with me.

And now, of course, our paths have crossed again and will forever be linked thanks to this single.

But does that mean anything for us, him and me? Or am I reading way too much into this?

I dismiss the whisper of hope that blooms in my chest as I glance at him across the booth, headphones on as we wait for the sound techs, and he gives me a saucy wink.

I hide my smile behind a sip of water and swallow the butterflies in my stomach.

"Ready?" the tech asks into our headphones, and I shift my attention back to the task at hand, rather than the absurd daydreams running through my mind.

"Ready."

AN HOUR LATER, IT'S a wrap, and we listen to the rough cut with Ben and the rest of the band in the control room.

"You sound amazing," Cole murmurs in my ear as everyone smiles and nods along, pleased with how the song turned out.

"I could pinch myself right about now," I admit in a whisper, turning to meet his eyes.

"Me, too."

"Macy," Ben says, drawing my attention back to the group before I can process what Cole means. "We'll be in touch with your agent to talk promo ops and schedule some PR performances as early as the beginning of March. It's already been a few months, but we think the window to act is still wide open, and we want to jump on the momentum the video has created, you know, and capture the audience."

"Sounds good," I say with a nod.

"Oh, and the label wants to open negotiations for a contract, if you're interested."

If I'm interested? In a contract with a major record label, a label that's signed Heartwood and a dozen other chart-topping country artists?

"Yes, of-of course," I stammer, cursing myself for not being cool, calm, and collected. "Thanks again—for everything—but I've got to go."

I shake hands with Ben, wave goodbye at everyone else who helped today, grab my purse off the chair, and turn to leave, certain my face is flushed.

"I'll walk you out." Cole's warm hand lands lightly on the small of my back and steadies me. It feels...nice.

Out in the hallway, I glance at my phone, calculating how long it will take to get to the sitters from here.

We fall in step on my way toward the elevator, and Cole shoots me a sidelong glance. "Can I take you two to dinner?"

"Two?"

"You and Mason."

Oh.

"Tonight?" I squeak, blurting out the first thing that comes to mind.

He lifts a shoulder. "Unless you have other plans."

"No, I—we don't. Hannah and Hunter are coming for the weekend, but they won't be here until close to midnight."

"Great."

"No, I..." I trail off, debating how to phrase the rejection while still keeping my options open with Cole.

"You don't want to introduce me to Mason."

My steps falter, and I catch myself, but not before he reaches out an arm to steady me. An arm that remains until we approach the elevator, and I meet his eyes. He doesn't seem upset, rather stating the facts as he sees them and not taking it personally. And he's right.

"It's not you, really. It's just that I don't bring men home—ever."

"Never in five years?"

I shake my head, almost embarrassed to admit I'm so inexperienced. "Not once."

His eyes narrow. "So that night, in Atlanta, on my bus..."

I nod, confirming his assumption. "It was my first time in almost six years, and only my second time ever."

He rubs a hand over his stubble-covered cheeks, amazement slackening his expression as the elevator dings, and I escape inside.

He follows. "I'm going to take that as a compliment, Macy Porter. I only wish I'd known the privilege you were giving me at the time."

My pulse races at the direction this conversation is taking, and I word vomit, unable to contain my explanation. "It was great, really. You did...well. I just thought it would be one night, you know? Just a hot fling and nothing more. And it was until..."

"New Year's." He nods, and his dark eyes study me as if he's solving a mystery in real time. As if a disjointed harmony is coming together in his mind. "You didn't only run that morning because of Mason, but because I showed up in the first place."

I press my lips together and nod. *Bingo.*

The elevator doors slide open, and I escape again, jetting toward the exit at the front of the building and shooting a quick glance at the uniformed security guard.

"Macy, wait."

I freeze at the command, but not because of the words. Because of the tone. Cole's voice is urgent with a touch of desperation.

He rounds in front of me in the empty lobby and reaches for both of my hands, clasping them in his own. "Macy, look, you have every right to walk away. You don't owe me anything, and hell, based on my reputation, I wouldn't blame you. But I haven't slept with anyone since that night in December. And I didn't track you down all the way in Kissing Springs on New Year's Eve for just another night, another roll in bed. I needed to find *you*, to see you again, because I couldn't get you out of my mind. You're kind and beautiful and amazing and that morning—learning you have a son—changed nothing. It only made me respect you more."

"Cole—"

"No," he says, raising my hands and pressing a kiss to the knuckles on each one. "Please, let me explain. I didn't invite you here today just to record the song. The tour wrapped two days ago, and I wanted to see if there's even a sliver of a possibility you'll give me a chance to prove whatever's here between us, whatever *this* is, is more than just physical. Hell, if I have to, I won't sleep with you for a month to prove it. It wouldn't be easy because you're as sexy as hell, and I want to kiss you again right now, but—"

I cut him off by pressing up on my toes and kissing him. He releases my hands and crushes me to him with a groan, his fingers weaving through my hair, and he wastes no time deepening the kiss.

His tongue skates along my bottom lip, and I open for him, knowing full well I'm opening my world, too. Cole Heartwood might be the death of me, might break my heart into a million pieces, but if I don't give whatever *this* is—if I don't give him—a chance, I'll never know.

"Macy," he murmurs against my lips, before pulling away and blowing out a long breath. "I'm never going to make it through dinner if we keep this up."

I smirk and grab the waistband of his jeans. "I thought you said you wouldn't sleep with me for a month."

"Did I say that?" he says, pretending not to remember and shooting me one of his famous smiles.

"Yes, and I think that's up for negotiation, but for now, how about dinner at my place, and I can introduce you to Mason—as my friend?"

"I'd be honored. Plus," he adds, a flicker of amusement dancing through his eyes, "If we're at your house, you won't be able to slip away."

16

Cole

"IT'S BEEN A LONG time since I had macaroni and cheese, but that was delicious." I can't remember the last time I had a homecooked meal or ate dinner at a worn wooden table pressed up against a wall in the kitchen, just like at my grandpa's house.

"You missed a pea." Mason points at the three-compartment plate he insisted I use. "You have to eat all your veggies if you want a treat. Plus, we don't waste food in this house." He says the last bit in a tone that tells me he's heard that declaration a time or two.

"That's a good policy. I always had to eat my vegetables when I was a little boy, too."

I didn't really, but I don't want to ruffle any feathers. I glance across the small, wooden table at Macy. Her lips are pressed together as if to hide a smile, and she doesn't meet my eyes.

"But not anymore?" Mason's face scrunches up as if there's a loophole he hasn't quite figured out, and Macy rushes to set the record straight.

"Mr. Heartwood still eats all of his veggies now because they help keep his body healthy," she says pointedly, now looking at me.

I scoop up the pea with my spoon, popping it into my mouth, and assure him I do, in fact, eat my vegetables now.

"But Mason," Macy says, "don't you think all the sweets you had at the party at school should count for your treat today?"

His little head, full of dark curls, just like his mom's, shakes vigorously. "But it's Friday... and those were at school."

She seems to consider his plea for a minute. "Remember, Hannah and Hunter are coming to visit, and tomorrow is Valentine's Day, so I'm sure there will be more goodies then."

"They'll be here when I wake up?"

"They will."

"Okay," he says, "but we can still have popcorn during the movie, right? After all, it's a special night because you have a friend over."

"Movie?" I ask, looking from Mason to Macy and back.

Mason nods. "Anytime Mommy's home on Friday night, we watch a movie together after our macaroni and cheese."

Macy lifts a shoulder. "It's kind of tradition."

"Well, don't let me change your plans—"

"You're not leaving, are you?" Mason cries, his eyes darting from me to Macy and back. "You can't leave now!"

"I'm happy to stay and watch a movie, if you don't mind."

"I don't mind," Mason insists, shaking his little head again. "You don't mind, either, do you, Mom?"

"No, honey, I don't mind, either," Macy says, meeting my eyes.

Mason springs up and clears his plate to the counter by the sink while I sink into Macy's intent look.

"Honey, why don't you go get your PJs on while Mr. Heartwood and I clean up?"

"Okay." He jets out of the room at full speed.

"He's great." I rise to clear my plate.

"Thanks, I try."

"I can tell. He's lucky to have you."

Together, we clear the dishes, and our hands brush a few times, thanks to the close quarters.

"That wasn't too bad, was it?" I ask.

"What?"

"Introducing me to Mason? Having me for dinner?"

"No," she admits with a tiny lift of her shoulder. "It was...nice."

"And you turned me back on to macaroni and cheese. I'll have to tell Tessa to order it for me, sometimes."

"Tessa's your PA, right?"

"And still not someone I've slept with," I say, harkening back to our conversation that first night on my bus when Tessa's name came up and Macy jumped to conclusions.

"Have you promoted her yet?"

"You have an excellent memory, but no, not yet."

At the dishwasher, Macy continues loading, but noticeably slower. I bide my time, waiting for her to share whatever she's pondering. Sure enough, a minute later, she spins to face me, and my stomach drops at the resolved look on her face.

"I thought it was nice to have me here." I hold up both hands and try to calm the alarm wrenching my gut.

"It was... It is. It's just that I like you, and I don't want you to think I'm only having you over—only wanting to spend time with you—because you're Cole Heartwood."

Another hang up. One I need to dissuade her of right now.

"Macy, sweetheart, believe me when I tell you the thought has never crossed my mind. Hell, if anything, I'm the one who's pursued you."

I step closer and brush a stray hair that's escaped from her ponytail back behind her ear. "There've been more than a few folks over the years who have tried to use me for one thing or another, and I've learned to spot it a million miles away. You couldn't be more different."

She sighs and looks up at me, doubt still etched on her face. "You're sure?"

"I'm sure. Plus, Ben mentioned a contract earlier, so it's probably only a matter of time until you're a bigger star than me."

She scoffs and shakes her head, her ponytail swinging, but I meet her eyes. She studies me for a minute, her lips pressing together, but then she opens her mouth and says, "There's something else, too."

My heart skips a beat. *Something else?*

"What?"

She glances off and wrings her hands together. "I know earlier, in the lobby, you said you think there's something between us, something *more*, but..."

"But you don't believe me."

She lifts a shoulder. "I don't know what to believe."

This is a hell of my own making, and I don't blame her for questioning my intentions.

"Macy, I—"

"No, let me speak, please." She paces back and forth, even though it's not more than three steps in each direction across the kitchen and back.

"Look, Cole, I'm not judging you for anything you've done—heaven knows, I've made my share of bad choices—and I knew what I was getting into that first night on the bus, believe me, I did. But now, you're here, in my house, and I've introduced you to my son. I just need to know I'm not going to wake up tomorrow and see another headline or read another story about your latest arm candy. I need to know, at least while we're figuring this out, that it's just us...you and me."

She stills and turns to me, clear resolve in her eyes. She's willing to say goodbye forever tonight, to end this once and for all, and I don't blame her. But what she doesn't know is, I couldn't imagine wanting another woman again. Ever. Which is something I'm still coming to grips with myself.

"Macy, I wouldn't have come over tonight, and there's no way in hell I would have had you introduce me to your son, if there was even a sliver of doubt in my mind. I—"

She opens her mouth to speak, but I step toward her and reach for her hand.

"I can't control what people say about me, or what they publish, but you can always believe what I say is the truth, I promise."

"That's what Ben said, too."

"Ben?"

"The first time I saw you onstage, during the sound check you gave a little speech to the kids, you know, from the Atlanta Children's Choir."

"Okay." I draw the word out because I have no idea where this is going.

"It didn't quite jive with who I thought Cole Heartwood was, the type of guy you were, the man I was expecting based on everything I'd read. But Ben was there, backstage, and he said you always say what you mean."

I nod. "My grandpa would've had my hide if he thought for an instant I was being anything less than honest."

There's a touch of a smile on her lips. "I believe you, Cole, and until you do something to break my trust, I'll keep believing what you say."

"Promise?"

"I promise." She shoots a glance at the doorway. "And I really want to kiss you right now, but can you wait about an hour? Mason'll be out like a light by then."

"I'm waiting a month, remember?"

She does a double take then catches my expression, rolls her eyes and laughs. "Then I'll be the one doing the kissing."

We'll see about that.

17

Macy

Cole stands next to my piano by the window when I return from tucking in Mason. The sharp contours of his familiar jaw and long lashes are illuminated by the golden glow of the streetlight outside.

His fingers run along the silent keys, and he seems to take stock of my stack of notebooks piled high on the shelf above, and the disorderly jumble of half-filled sheets of music on the stand, along with a few pink, red, and white Valentine's Day decorations.

"See anything interesting?" I ask, stepping into the room.

"Yeah, everything."

"I'm sure that's not true." I make my way to his side.

"It is. Especially, now that you're back."

"And alone," I murmur, because although my pulse races and I'm not sure how this dating thing works, my body, which has been attuned to Cole's presence ever since he greeted me at the studio this afternoon, aches with need.

He meets my eyes and seems to study my expression. "Not quite."

"What?"

He draws me a few steps away from the window, and when I shoot him a questioning glance, he points to a black SUV parked on the street outside. "We've got company."

"Security?"

"My bodyguard."

"He was there, too, on New Year's Eve, or morning, as it were. In Kissing Springs."

Hannah had pulled back the curtains to point him out.

"He's always there, but yes, Steven spent the night outside your cousin's place."

I suppose it comes with the territory, with dating someone famous enough to need a bodyguard. My stomach churns, but I push the racing thoughts from my mind. There's time enough to consider what I'm getting into another time.

My tongue darts out to moisten my lips. Not because I'm trying to be sexy, but because my mouth is as dry as the desert out west. "Time for that kiss, I promised," I say, trying for casual.

"My lips are right here." A mischievous gleam twinkles in Cole's eyes as he points to his tempting lips.

I arch an eyebrow. "Think I need directions?"

He reaches for me, resting a hand on my hip, and his look transforms from playful to intense in an instant. "Macy, you're the most beautiful, most talented, most competent woman I've ever met. The last thing you need is anything from a man like me."

I lift on my bare toes and wrap my arms around his neck. "Tonight, I'll just take you."

"I like the sound of that," he growls, the words humming low and deep in his chest.

I press my lips to his as warmth unfurls through my body, a sense of conviction that this man at my side is sincere and everything I didn't know I was looking for.

The sensation releases a need for him, racing through my core and landing at the juncture between my thighs. His hands cup my ass and pull me against him, against his erection, and a moan escapes my throat at the touch and the knowledge he wants me.

I squirm against him, seeking friction, and tilt my head, parting my lips and granting him access. He claims my mouth with another groan that reverberates through our clothes, teasing the sensitive tips of my nipples, which harden.

"Cole," I murmur, breaking away and meeting his dark eyes. "Please."

"You sure?"

For an instant, I don't understand why he's asking, why he's hesitating, but his eyes flick to the doorway, toward the hallway where Mason's sleeping.

And I get his hesitation, appreciate it even, as it echoes my own concerns from earlier today. But now that he's here, his body pressed against mine, there's no way I want to stop.

"I'll be quiet. I promise."

He flashes a wicked grin.

"I wish I could take that as a challenge, but I'll save it for another time," he whispers.

I grab his hand and lead him to my bedroom, which, thankfully, doesn't share a wall with Mason's room. I hold the handle and silently close the door, turning the lock, and then spin to meet his heated gaze.

"Ever since New Year's, I've thought about you," I admit, pulling out my hair tie and releasing my ponytail so my curls cascade down my back.

He grabs the hem of his long-sleeved shirt and draws it off over his head, tossing it aside on the floor. "Tell me what you did when you thought about me, Macy."

His tone is low and commanding, as if he's asked a question he already knows the answer to but wants to hear me say it.

The throbbing between my legs intensifies. "I…I made myself come."

His eyebrow arches, and he waves a finger at me to remove my sweater. "Tell me more."

I drag my sweater over my head and stand before him in my bra, enjoying the lazy way his eyes roam down my body. "I thought of my night with you on the bus, remembered the things you did to me, and I touched myself."

"Watching you touch yourself is another *activity* I'll have to file away for a later date." He unbuttons his jeans and slides them off along with his boxers and stands naked before me.

And what a sight he is. Wide shoulders and thick pecs lead down to rippled abs and the crowning jewel, his cock extending out in front of him. My breath catches as I stare, but his next question, and especially the seductive tone, sends my gaze back up to his face. "Did you use a toy? Something you pretended was me?"

A flush creeps up my neck, and I glance away, but Cole steps forward and lifts my chin with a single finger. "Please tell me yes. And please, tell me it felt good. Even if I wasn't here to pleasure you, I want to know you enjoyed the memory of when I fucked you."

I bite my lip and nod. "I did."

His jaw clenches, and his eyes close for a minute. "Just thinking of you, here alone, touching yourself, when I was doing the same thing… It makes me want to make up for lost time."

I try to drop to my knees, eager to take him in my mouth, but he stops me with his hands on my shoulders.

"No." He eases the sting of rejection with a kiss and presses his forehead to mine. "I haven't forgotten that I owe you."

My brow wrinkles against his. "Owe me?"

He drops to his knees and starts undoing my pants, drawing them down my legs. "Do you remember, at that bar in Kissing Springs on New Year's Eve? I promised to lick you and make you come."

My knees quiver at the sear of his fingers on my skin, and I grab his shoulders for balance. My memories from that night are hazy at best. "You did?"

"Mm-hmm." He presses a kiss to my heat over my underwear. I gasp as he murmurs, "I did."

"Oh."

He draws my underwear down, too, and spreads my legs, holding an ankle with each hand. My thighs squeeze together—or try to.

"Cole," I whisper, my nails digging into his shoulder blades. "Please."

"Please, what? Tell me what you want."

"Please, lick me. I need you to lick me now."

He looks up at me through long lashes, and for a second, I think he's going to tease me more, but instead, he issues a warning. "Remember, you're going to keep quiet, right?"

"Yes." I nod emphatically, desperate for his touch.

He points to the bed. "Lie down."

A minute later, his tongue swipes through my folds and caresses my clit. I bite back a moan as my thighs tremble and every fiber of my being focuses on the sensation, on the pressure and the pleasure. His hands grip my thighs and then curve around and cup my ass, holding me tight against his unrelenting mouth.

Until it's too much.

"Cole, I'm coming. I'm coming," I whisper-hiss, although I'm sure he doesn't need my announcement. My juices flow over his face as I tense, and every muscle in my body shudders.

And then, before I know it, he's on top of me, nuzzling my neck. "Good girl."

My hands skate down his chest, and I scoot down to reach for his cock, encircling it with one hand while I cup his balls with the other. A muscle in his jaw works, and his baritone voice is tight. "Macy."

"Cole, please."

He shifts off, only long enough to roll on a condom before he's there again, in place, poised above me, every muscle in his body tense.

"You sure?" He looks me in the eye.

I nod. "I'm sure."

18

Macy

Mason's quick footsteps in the hallway, followed by the jingle from Daisy's collar, bring me from sound asleep to wide awake in an instant. Fortunately, Hunter's groggy voice greets my son, and the back door opens and closes, the house falling silent again as they take Hunter's dalmatian outside to our postage-stamp sized backyard.

I roll over, my body languid from the ministrations of a certain country star last night, a man who can play my body as well as he plays the guitar, and heave a contented sigh.

Although a million questions float through my mind, at least one thing is clear this morning. Cole's in this, whatever *this* is. He made certain I understood that before he left last night, and I promised to give it, give us, a chance—a real chance—too.

I grab my phone off the nightstand and bite back a smile at the sight of a text from Cole, sent just after midnight.

Thanks again for dinner and the movie. And especially for after.

Rustling in the kitchen catches my ear, and I shoot back a quick text.

Thanks for the company. I enjoyed every minute and can't wait for those 'activities' you filed away for another time.

I scramble up to sitting, wondering what his response will be, and throw on a robe. In the kitchen there's a pot of coffee brewing, and Hannah is searching through the cupboard.

"Good morning."

"Happy Valentine's Day," she says, spinning to face me with a wide smile.

"You're up early for a woman who pulled into my driveway just after midnight."

"I slept in the car while Hunter drove," she says, by way of explanation. "But I promised Mason I'd make red velvet pancakes when I visited. Sorry, I forgot to mention it before now."

I wave off her apology. "We should have everything you need. Mason and I just made homemade chocolate chip cookies a few weeks ago."

She dips her chin toward a wrapped item on the table. "I brought something for you, from Mrs. McArthur."

I eye it suspiciously, and Hannah chuckles, catching my look.

"Do you know what it is?" I pick up the brown-paper wrapped gift.

"I can guess. I've been on the receiving end of a few of Mrs. McArthur's *gifts* myself."

I tug on the twine and rip off the wrapping to find a paperback with a bare-chested man with a guitar on the cover. "*Her Rockstar Valentine*."

Hannah lifts a shoulder. "It tracks. She asked about the SUV parked outside on New Year's Eve after rumor spread around town about a *certain country heartthrob* making a surprise appearance at the Bourbon Boot Scoot."

I tuck the paperback in a drawer and grab three mugs from the cabinet, but before I form a response, the back door creaks open, and Daisy's collar jingles again as she trots down the hallway.

"Morning." Hunter comes in, shooting me a smile before he fills a water dish for Daisy.

"Where's Mason?" I ask, peering toward the doorway.

"He went to his room to grab a new Hot Wheels. Said he couldn't wait to show it to me."

"Oh." I swallow at Hunter's gleeful tone because I know where this is going.

Hunter catches Hannah's eye. "He said Mr. Heartwood gave it to him last night when he came over for dinner and a movie."

"Macy Porter!" Hannah exclaims, her jaw dropping as she meets my eyes. "Cole was here? Last night? Are you seeing him?"

"Shh," I whisper-hiss, glancing toward the doorway again. "Mr. Heartwood is just a friend—at least, as far as Mason is concerned."

"That's going to last a whole five seconds," Hunter mutters, cocking an eyebrow at Hannah.

"He's right." She draws me to the table to sit down next to her, the pancakes momentarily forgotten. "Mason's got a sixth sense about this kind of thing. He'll be onto you before you know it. You need to tell him."

I run a hand through my hair. "But I've never brought home a man. I don't want to introduce him to someone just to have the guy gone in a matter of weeks."

"A, you already introduced him, even if it was just *as friends*."

I scrunch my nose. "And B?"

"B, do you think Cole will be gone in a matter of weeks? He tracked you down on New Year's Eve and drove hundreds of miles, for heaven's sake. Plus, you didn't see his face that morning when I had to tell him you were gone."

I pick at an imaginary piece of lint on the red, heart-shaped placemat on the table. "I don't think he'll be gone in a matter of weeks."

And not just because of the single we're about to release.

"See? If you think there's something there, you should let Mason in on it. His relationship with Cole will be just as important as his relationship with you."

She's right.

"You're right. I will soon. It's just that I'm still trying to...to figure it all out myself."

"When are you going to see him again?"

"About that..."

"What?" she says, drawing out the word and arching an eyebrow in my direction.

"Any chance you two might be interested in watching Mason for me tonight?"

Mason pops through the doorway just in time to answer for them, his voice squeaky with excitement. "Hannah and Daddy are going to watch me tonight? *Yesssss!*"

"We'd be happy to," Hannah says, in a tone that says she knows exactly what's going to happen tonight on my date. "And I hope you have a great time on Valentine's Day. You deserve it."

MARCH | NEW YORK CITY

There's just something bout the morning that make each day a joy to see
The nighttime brings a peaceful feeling that rests inside of me
I love you please believe me,
I won't want you to ever leave me
But I was raised on country sunshine
~ Country Sunshine by Dottie West

19

Cole

I DON'T, AS THEY say, love New York. I tolerate it. But the Big Apple is where the label decided we should launch the new single, and when Macy found out, she lit up brighter than a Christmas tree strung with dozens of strands of twinkle lights.

She'd never been before and proceeded to tell me all the things she wanted to do in the city. Her enthusiasm was infectious. Especially, when I considered the potential of a two-night stay in the city that never sleeps. Alone. With her.

"Is the suite to your liking, Mr. Heartwood? Is there anything I can have brought up for you?" Tessa's voice comes through the computer speaker as professional as always.

"Has she touched down yet?"

"Give me one moment."

I rock back on my heels and shove my hands in my back pockets. I can't wait for Macy to see the view of the city, lit up in the dark, from this spot on the twenty-first floor of The Plaza.

Tessa checks whatever she checks for that kind of information while Ben paces in the adjoining dining area on a call.

"Approximately two minutes ago, sir."

Sure enough, my phone on the coffee table buzzes. I beeline for it and can't help but smile at Macy's text that lights up my screen.

Flying into NYC at night might just be my new favorite thing. Even more than the warm nuts they served with my sparkling water.

"Warm nuts, hmm?"

"What's that, sir?"

I glance at the laptop, but Tessa's expression gives nothing away. She heard what I said, but my PA would never admit it. She's efficient, competent, and, most importantly, discreet. Which, over the past few years, I've needed. And still do, but now, for different reasons.

"Nothing. Everything is fine. The room is fine. The champagne is here on ice."

"Very well then. Would you like me to review the schedule with you for tomorrow?"

"Sure." I sink onto the couch and drag over my guitar case.

"The car will be waiting at seven a.m. to take you, Macy, and Ben to the Rise and Shine studio. Steven will move with you, of course, and manage his team. The band and tech crew will travel separately and should be set up and ready to go when you arrive."

I undo the latches on my case and flip open the lid as she continues, double checking that the folded piece of paper with the lyrics I've been workshopping is still tucked under my guitar where I left it.

"The performance will be in the nine o'clock hour with the joint interview in the next segment. Melissa will be there, as well, to ensure everything goes smoothly."

"Melissa?"

Ben, who's finished his call, answers first as he takes a seat in an upholstered armchair by the fireplace. "You remember, the new PR director from the label."

Oh, yeah. "The one who wants me to *play up* my relationship with Macy."

Ben cocks an eyebrow but remains silent while Tessa wisely ignores my outburst.

"From there, you—" she continues, but I cut her off.

"Did you make the dinner reservations for tomorrow night?"

"Yes, sir, exactly as you requested," Tessa replies, not missing a beat.

"Good." I strum a G7 chord, look down at my fingers, and shift to a Dm7.

"At Fourteen Park Avenue?" Ben asks, running a hand down his beard.

I ignore his tone, which suggests more than mere curiosity. "Yes."

"Just the two of you?" he presses, and I tighten my hold on the neck of my guitar.

"Yes."

My response invites no further questions, but the conversation is far from over, and we both know it. I couldn't care less that the label believes confirming the speculation about my relationship with Macy will, as they say, be good for sales. As close as we've gotten and as much as I'd like to, I'm not ready to go public, to make it official.

Quiet settles in the room for a moment, and then Tessa, completely unruffled, continues. "After the interview segment, you'll move on to The Late Showdown, which tapes at two. From there, it's to the photoshoot for the magazine cover at four. Once that wraps, you'll be free for the evening."

"Perfect."

"I'll be in contact with both of you tomorrow, but don't hesitate to—."

"I know, I know... Reach out if there's anything I need."

"Or if there's anything I can do for Ms. Porter, of course."

For a second, I wonder if Tessa was given instructions to support Macy, too, but I dismiss the thought as soon as it appears. Tessa is loyal and has proven time and time again she doesn't judge anyone. Many times, without comment, she's assisted women who needed something when they were with me, sometimes even before they asked.

I haven't told my PA how serious Macy and I are, but surely, she's noticed there hasn't been another woman since December. And that I've spent every spare moment with Macy since Valentine's Day.

"Thanks, Tessa."

"Yeah, thanks, Tessa," Ben adds, looking up from his phone.

"Macy should be arriving within twenty minutes. The car just turned onto Grand Central Parkway. Enjoy the trip, gentlemen."

She disconnects, and I play for a few minutes until Ben clears his throat and sets his phone on the coffee table.

"What?"

He leans back and crosses one leg over the other at the knee. "As much as you don't want to admit it, you know they're right."

"Who's right?"

He waves a hand through the air. "The label, PR... Hell, anyone who has a vested interest in your success."

I grit my teeth. We've been through this before. "My relationship with Macy is not something to be *managed*."

"I know you say that, but you've been in the business long enough to know, when you're as famous as Cole Heartwood, and worth as much as you are, everyone has an opinion, especially the folks who sign your checks."

"I'm done being managed. They didn't seem to mind when I made headlines with a new woman every week, and now, when *they* want me to be exclusive because it will be good for sales, they think I'm just going to give in, just like that?"

He opens his mouth, but I barrel on. "Macy and I have a good thing going, and I'm not about to ruin it by going public."

He runs a hand through his hair. "The release is tomorrow, and it's only a matter of time. Hell, you two have been together for weeks now. What's the holdup?"

When I don't provide an answer, Ben continues, leaving forward, elbows on his knees. "Look, we've got an opportunity tomorrow, and all we're saying—"

I press the flat of my hand to my strings to silence them. "Wait. *We?*"

He heaves a sigh and rises, grabbing a bottle of water from the sideboard. "Yes, we. Me, included. Look, Cole, you know I wouldn't be encouraging you to go public with Macy if I didn't think there was something there between you."

I grit my teeth. There is something there, but it's been just the two of us, with Mason, for the past few weeks. It's a bubble I've enjoyed, and I don't want to burst.

"When we decide to make it official, it'll be on our terms, not thanks to some choreographed PR stunt meant to impact sales—"

"Sales that will help her career, too, Cole. You can't ignore that. Plus, anyone who's watched even ten seconds of that video from Atlanta can see it didn't go viral because of the amazing sound quality. It went viral because of the chemistry between you two."

I scoff and set my guitar back in its case and snap shut the lid. "Chemistry the label hopes to capitalize on—at least, while the single is topping the charts."

Ben takes a long swig of water and heaves a sigh. "You know it'll make headlines, but in a good way. Look, I know you've never been one to commit to much of anything, but don't you think Macy deserves to be confirmed as your girlfriend? Until it's official, you're opening her up to speculation about where she stands with you."

I shake my head, unable to give in, no matter how right he might be. Not that I could say exactly why, but something is holding me back.

"No," I say, finally, low and resolute. "It's not fair to either of us to *play up* our relationship or go public just because it's what's best for the label. This time, no managing, no staging, no lies. My personal life and my relationship will be on my terms. And hers."

20

Macy

What kind of hotel room has a doorbell? The kind you'd find at The Plaza, apparently. I stare at it while Steven, Cole's head of security, nods at the burly guard in a dark suit stationed outside the door. Then, he raps twice with the old-fashioned knocker and breezes into the suite, without waiting for an answer.

"You have a suite, as well," Steven says over his shoulder as we pass through the foyer. "But Mr. Heartwood requested I escort you here upon arrival."

Of course, he did. Ever since Valentine's Day, Cole and I have spent time together, usually at my place and often with Mason. The two of them have become close, which is great, but I worry about what will happen when this is all over.

But that's a problem for another day. For now, this trip, a PR blitz for the release of the single, is a chance for Cole and me to spend some time together. Alone.

Or as alone as Cole ever is, which is to say, never. Steven has spent more than his fair share of nights parked in an SUV on the street in front of my house.

I hear Cole before I see him, strumming the melody from an old Willie Nelson song on his guitar. The notes stop abruptly as we make our way through a dining area to a sitting room where Cole is alone, lounging on a couch in front of an enormous fireplace, looking as sexy as ever in his ripped jeans.

"Mr. Heartwood." Steven nods, but Cole barely acknowledges him. He only has eyes for me. He sets his guitar aside and rises, raking me from head to toe with a look that's half *you're a sight for sore eyes* and half *I want to rip those clothes off your body*.

The combination is lethal, and my steps falter and come to a stop as Cole pulls me into his arms. He presses a soft, lingering kiss on my lips that heats my blood and leaves me breathless.

Steven turns and departs, his leather loafers clicking on the wood floor.

"Do you always send your head of security to transport a guest from the airport to the hotel?"

I say it in jest, but Cole draws back and meets my eyes, his expression grave. "Never."

Oh.

"But you're no guest."

I'm glad we agree on that, even if we haven't determined exactly what we are. This morning, when I dropped off Mason in Kissing Springs, Hannah asked me again what exactly our status is, and I didn't have a good answer, instead falling back to the generic, 'It's complicated.' She gave me a look I didn't want to examine too closely, and I changed the subject.

As if he can read my mind, Cole asks, "Did everything go okay with dropping Mason off?"

I nod. "He's settled in Kissing Springs, as happy as a clam with Hannah and Hunter. Plus, he can't wait for you to come with me to pick him up, so he can show you around."

"I'm looking forward to visiting Kissing Springs for more than eight hours. I've heard good things about the music scene there and the venue. What's it called again?"

"The Boyd Theater. If it was there six years ago, I might not have had to move to Nashville to follow my dreams."

Not that I didn't want to get out of town for other reasons, but Cole knows the story, and why I have the policy I enacted on New Year's Eve. A policy I don't know if I'll ever need again.

"Dreams that are coming true," Cole says quietly, meeting my eyes. I'm not sure he's talking about my career, but before I can agree, he asks, "Can I get you anything? Are you thirsty? Hungry? We can order up anything you'd like."

"I'm good, thanks. I had those warm nuts, remember?"

My lips twitch until he rocks his hips against me and growls, "That's not enough sustenance for what I have in mind for you tonight."

It's as if the words, in his low, slow drawl, are addressed directly to my lady parts. My thighs clench in delicious anticipation, and I lick my lips. "Tell me more."

"Well," he begins, with a twinkle in his eye. "I seem to remember a few activities I filed away for later."

I remember.

I slip my arms around his waist. "It's later now."

"Sure is."

"What did you have in mind?"

He tucks a strand of hair behind my ear. "What's the opposite of keeping quiet? That's what I have in mind."

"I'm on board, but..."

"But what?"

My eyes flick toward the entryway. "You have security right outside the door, standing guard."

His eyebrows come together. "And?"

Cole is unflustered by the notion someone will hear us and realization dawns. I swallow hard and tug away.

"What is it, Macy?"

His tone demands an answer, but I spin and move to the coffee table. I set down my purse and shrug off my coat, buying a minute.

"What?" he asks, softer this time.

I don't meet his eyes but stare into the empty fireplace. "He's heard it all before, hasn't he? Maybe not him exactly, but...but them." I wave my hand toward the front door.

It's easy to forget Cole is *the* Cole Heartwood when we're hanging out in my family room playing Candyland or watching Seinfeld reruns, but suddenly, the fact he earned his playboy reputation threatens to close my throat because I'm still technically one of a long list of women, even if our tryst has lasted longer than most.

"Yes," he says, not missing a beat. "They've heard it all before. But not since that night in December when I met you, Macy."

His voice is tight, but he doesn't understand. I spin to face him.

"I'm not accusing you of anything, Cole. I believe you. But the rumors about us have been flying, and they're only bound to get worse with the release—"

"They're not rumors, Macy. It's the truth. We are together. At least, I thought we were." His hands curl into fists, but he doesn't move. His feet are planted, and he's watching me.

I eye the tall windows that cover almost two full walls and make my way toward them, trying to gather my thoughts. This isn't how I wanted this trip to start.

The view from here is almost as breathtaking as the one from the air. The bright lights of New York City at night reach high above our height on the twenty-first floor and go on as far as the eye can see, but I'm too agitated to appreciate them.

Maybe, it's the trip and my anxiety about the performances and the release tomorrow, but I can't seem to find the words to explain how I feel or what I want.

After a minute, Cole steps up behind me. He doesn't touch me, but our eyes meet in the reflection in the glass. His presence is reassuring. I blow out a long breath, but my voice is still brittle when I finally speak.

"We are together. At least, I want to be. Hell, I've never been more together with a man in my life, but—"

"But you want to earn your success and not have it credited to the fact you're dating Cole Heartwood."

"Yes, but also..." I trail off, hesitant to voice a concern I confessed to Hannah only hours ago, after she showed me yet another headline that speculated on my relationship with Cole. An article predicted he'd be on to a new flavor of the month before Memorial Day and proceeded to name the top contenders, including a model, two actresses, and an up-and-coming female country artist. Like me.

But the concern isn't new. It's lurked in the back of my mind since last month and plagued me for the entire flight here. Especially because of the way we met. Well, not met exactly, but the way I jumped into his bed that first night.

Half of me wonders if perhaps the novelty hasn't quite worn off yet for Cole, especially after I slipped away—twice.

He places a hand on my hip and murmurs, "But also, what, sweetheart?"

I spin to face him and square my shoulders. "I don't want to be just another notch on your belt. I'm waiting for the day when you grow tired of me and move on, and...and I'm trying not to think about how I'll feel when that happens, because every day, every time, we spend time together and I lose to you at Scrabble or you quote the exact same song lyric I was thinking of..." I swallow the lump in my throat. "Every time, you play Hot Wheels with Mason or eat your vegetables at dinner, so he will, too, I lose a little bit of my heart to you and—"

He cuts me off with a kiss. The press of his lips to mine steals the rest of my words and disperses them into thin air like a wisp of smoke from a tinder that doesn't catch the flame.

His hand cups my cheek and slides back to curl around the nape of my neck. And I can't help it. I close my eyes and melt into him, taking every ounce of reassurance he's giving. It fills me until there's no room for doubt.

"Macy," he murmurs against my lips, drawing away and pressing my head to his shoulder. I snuggle against him and wrap my arms around his waist. "It's not just you."

"What?"

"You said you've never been more together with a man in your life, and I know what you mean because I've never been more together with a woman like this, either. I've never felt the way I feel about you with anyone else."

He presses a kiss to my hair. "This is new for both of us, and we're meeting in the middle from two opposite directions, but that doesn't mean it can't work. It just means we have to be honest and trust each other. Plus," he says, with a sigh, "We have something else in common."

"We do?"

"Yup, except I've already got a taste of how it feels, and that's what scares me the most."

Wrinkles crease my brow. "A taste of what?"

"What it feels like to have you walk away, to slip off without a goodbye, and to think there's a chance it might be forever."

I never thought of it like that. "I'm sorry."

"Don't be." He draws back and tips my chin up. "You had good reasons to take off, and I don't blame you. But I hope you see how, if that doesn't prove I'm not going to be the one to walk away, then I don't know what else I can do to make you believe."

You could make it official, prove there's something between us besides the music. But I don't voice my concern. There's a reason he hasn't made us public, and despite his reassurances, I'm not sure I want to know what that reason is.

He gives me another kiss. "I know I said I was going to make you scream, but you don't have to worry that anyone will hear."

I cock an eyebrow. "Why's that?"

He tips his head toward an open stairway I see through a hallway across the room. "The bedroom is upstairs. Far away from prying ears."

I swallow my concerns for another night. After all, the blitz is only scheduled for a few days, so I'd better enjoy every minute with him now, while I can. There's a strong possibility that soon enough, Cole Heartwood might be just a musician I've collaborated with and nothing more.

I eye the staircase. "You must not realize how loud I can be."

It's his turn to be amused. "Actually, I was thinking screaming might not be good for your voice, with our performances tomorrow and all."

"Is the shower upstairs, too?"

His head falls to the side. "Yes."

"Any chance it has good acoustics?"

A slow, sexy smile curls his lips. "Only one way to find out."

21

Cole

Warm, fragrant steam fills the air and fogs the bathroom mirrors. I set the bottle of essential oil back in the basket by the oversized bathtub as Macy, already naked, slips into the stream of hot water falling from the ceiling-mounted rainfall showerhead.

She turns to see if I'm watching, as if I could tear my eyes away from the tempting sight. Slowly, with a sultry look that set me on fire, she runs her hands through her hair, then over her full breasts and pinches both nipples.

"You coming?" she asks as her hands slide south. "It's lonely in here."

I strip off my jeans and tug my shirt over my head, tossing both aside, then step in and haul her against me, claiming her mouth with a fierce kiss that betrays my need.

She grips my biceps as I wrap my arms around her waist and grab her ass, pulling her even closer.

Her curves are slick, and I run my hands over her tempting body. She moans softly when I kiss her earlobe and murmur, "Well, we can't have that, can we?"

Her fingernails dig into my shoulders, and she tilts her head, giving me access to trail kisses down to her collarbone. I hum with approval and wedge my leg between her thighs. She widens and rocks her pussy against my quad while her back arches, thrusting those tempting breasts against my chest. My hand skims up her side, and I draw back enough to cup her breast and flick a thumb over the taut nipple.

She gasps and meets my eyes, gazing at me through thick lashes. With a devilish grin, she slips her hand down my abs and grips my stiff cock. I suck in a sharp breath and close my eyes while she pumps me, her fingers sliding easily over my length in the hot water.

But tonight is about lavishing attention on her and giving her the affection she deserves, in a way I'm not free to do when Mason is only a room away.

With effort, I lift her hand away. "Any more of that and I'll be coming on your perfect skin instead of inside you, where I belong."

Her pout transforms to a sly smile, and with a murmur of approval, she glances down at my cock. "Now it's my turn to file that away as an *activity for later*."

A growl starts in my chest and hums from my throat at her words. My cock twitches, and I grit my teeth and step back, reaching for the loofah and bodywash to distract myself from the picture she's painted in my mind.

"Turn around. Put your hands flat on the wall and spread your legs."

She does as she's told but watches me over her shoulder as I squeeze the bodywash onto the loofah and rub it between my hands, the scented lather running down my arms.

"Now, how about those acoustics, hmm?" I step up behind her and run the loofah slowly down her spine to the top of her ass. She wiggles as a shiver runs through her, but instead of continuing on the path, I make lazy circles on her back. "Let's try you sing and I'll wash, but if you stop, I stop. Deal?"

"Deal," she agrees in a heartbeat.

After a few deep breaths, she begins, her voice low and soulful as she sings a song I've never heard. It's likely one she wrote, and for the hundredth time since we met, her talent astounds me.

While I enjoy the a cappella version and make a note to ask her about the song later, I fulfill my promise and wash every inch of her luscious body.

When I skim her breasts, the notes falter and her head falls back, but she doesn't stop. It's when I slide the loofah in between her legs that she trails off. Her forehead presses against the white tile while her legs tremble and her back arches. The movement sends her ass lifting toward me, and it rubs against my erection, the contact just enough to expel all of my self-control.

I drop the loofah and grab the handheld showerhead to my left, lifting it from its holder and rinsing the suds off her body from head to toe. I leave her pussy for last and place a steadying hand on her hip, as much for myself as for her, and aim the stream between her legs.

"Cole," she cries out. "Please, I need...more."

She doesn't need to ask twice. "Wait here," I growl. "Don't even think about moving."

In less than a minute, I'm back, my cock sheathed and throbbing. I grasp her hips and drag her back until she's bent over enough to take me. I press a hand between her shoulder blades, and she casts a look back at me, her eyes dark with lust.

"Ready?" I line up at her opening, the tip of my cock barely pressing into her.

Her eyes flutter closed, and she nods. "Yes, please, Cole. Now."

With a slow grind, I slide into her. She bites her lower lip, and the song lyrics from a moment ago are replaced by whimpers of pleasure that are music to my ears.

"Macy," I groan, holding steady deep within her as her inner muscles clench and release around me in a pulsing tempo.

I want to fuck her fast, hard, and deep, but I force myself to slow down. This is about her, her pleasure, and her need. I roll my hips, and she purrs, the sound reverberating around us.

I grit my teeth and thrust deeper, hitting her sweet spot. She's so wet and tight around me, her body trembling with the effort of holding still. I slip my hand down from her shoulder blades and around to find her clit, rubbing it as she moans and her hips start to rock. I continue my assault, keeping the pace nice and easy.

"I'm so close," she murmurs only seconds before she comes undone, her body pulsing around me as she cries out.

I hold still, filling her with my swollen cock as she comes down from her high, then I start up again, rocking into her faster and harder this time.

I slide my hand up her warm, slick skin from her thigh to her breast and pinch her nipple. Within seconds, she's back to the edge, pressing against the wall to thrust her hips back into me. "Harder, Cole. Give it to me."

I'm unable to resist her and couldn't deny her if I tried. I grab both of her hips and plow into her again and again.

"Yes," she groans, one hand slamming against the tile as I climax and call out her name, the release sending a shudder through me that steals my breath and fills my heart.

22

Macy

It's been a whirlwind of a morning, and it's only nine o'clock. Hannah texted half an hour ago, while I was in hair and makeup. She sent a picture of Mason in his solar system pajamas, eating a muffin and giving me a thumbs up. They had the show on already and looked forward to the performance.

There are nearly as many people backstage here at Rise and Shine, America's number one morning show, as there were in Atlanta for the stadium tour. The show's producer, whose name I've forgotten, is wearing a headset and uses her clipboard to weave through the throng.

"Is it always like this?" I ask, spotting Melissa, the PR rep from the studio, out of the corner of my eye. She's talking to Ashley Wood, the host of Rise and Shine, a drop-dead gorgeous, long-legged blonde who was made to be *On Air*.

"Only when we have guests like Cole Heartwood," the producer says over her shoulder while I trail behind her toward the open set ahead where the band is already situated. "No offense," she adds with a half-smile. "We're thrilled to have you, too."

"Of course," I murmur, wondering if she'd be singing a different tune if I were officially Cole's girlfriend.

A large digital clock on the wall with red block numbers shows less than ten minutes until our performance. Cole is ready to go under the bright lights, his signature mahogany acoustic guitar already around his neck. I shoot him a smile as the producer hands me off to a sound guy.

"Thank you," I call after her, but she's already scooted away.

"Nice boots."

I turn back to Cole, but before I can respond, Ben approaches, phone in hand. The barely contained excitement on his face silences us both.

"It's official. The single is number one."

My jaw drops while blood pounds in my ears. Pure disbelief races through me for a split second before I look at the phone he's holding up and see my name, next to Cole's, under the song title in the number one spot on the Billboard Chart. I feel faint seeing it there in black and white.

"Are you okay?" Cole's eyes search me, and he steps to my side, brushing away the sound tech. "Do you need some water?"

I fight the tears pricking at the back of my eyes and shake my head. "No, I'm... Yes, I'm okay. I just... I can't believe it."

A number one release was what everyone had expected, but for it to be real, for me, a struggling singer who, two years ago, was thrilled to perform the national anthem to a rowdy crowd waiting for kick-off and six months ago, would have been happy to hear a song of mine on the radio, it's a dream come true.

"I remember my first number one. It was surreal. It made every minute of the years of hustling and hard work worth it. But this one," he says, reaching for my hand and giving it a squeeze. "This one is special."

Ben clears his throat and slips his phone into his pocket. The hint of a frown flickers over his face, and his voice is curt when he says, "Congrats, both of you, really. Now, let's aim for platinum."

My stomach knots as Cole releases my hand, a muscle working in his jaw. My brow furrows, but he doesn't meet my eyes.

"Live in five." An announcement loud enough to be heard over the chatter triggers a flurry of activity. Cole pulls away as the sound tech returns, and I don't have a chance to examine what just happened.

I have my mic in hand and curl my fingers around it. I take a deep breath, trying to harness some of the nervous tension in my chest, as the producer, standing next to a camera, calls, "One minute until live."

A few feet in front of us, Ashley shoots us a smile and then turns back toward the teleprompter. She straightens her bright orange pencil skirt then squares her shoulders, and I wish I was half as composed as she is.

Cole leans away from his microphone toward me. He skims my back with his warm hand, and his breath brushes my cheek.

"You. Are. Perfect," he murmurs, his voice low and delicious.

And with that, the number one, the confusion, the disbelief, the knowledge that millions of people are watching right now... All of it melts away, and I meet Cole's dark eyes as the first notes of our duet play. It's just him and me, perfectly in sync, like that first time in Atlanta when the connection was electric even before either of us knew where that night would lead.

The performance is over in the blink of an eye. Cole holds my gaze until the last note fades and then winks at me as Ashley steps up next to us, a wide, perfect smile plastered on her face.

"Wow. That was amazing! I'm sure America can see why you two are topping the charts and setting the rumor mill on fire." She turns smoothly toward the camera. "Stay tuned because after these messages, we're going to hear firsthand from Cole Heartwood and Macy Porter about the viral video the internet just can't seem to get enough of and see if we can't get them to confirm there's more to their collaboration behind the scenes."

"And cut."

Before I can even take a breath, one of the hair and makeup staff approaches. She touches up my lipstick and adjusts my hair while Cole slips off his guitar and hands it to a stagehand.

Melissa, the PR person from the label I had a video call with yesterday on the plane, stands just behind the yellow line marked on the floor. She leans over to Ben, at her side, and whispers something to him, or maybe asks him a question. Either way, he shakes his head and rubs his chin before glancing up at Cole and me.

Once we're back *On Air,* the first few questions are ones we've practiced. I hold my own as far as answering without tripping over my words and hopefully appear more relaxed than I am.

But then Ashley leans in and lowers her voice. "Cole, I have to ask the question all of America is wondering, especially after they see the fireworks between you two, like this morning, here on Rise and Shine. Is there any truth to the rumor there's something more to your relationship than just professional collaboration?"

I freeze and make a concerted effort to maintain a neutral expression while Cole shifts at my side and, smooth as silk, says, "There have been many rumors about my relationships with women over the years that I've never confirmed or denied, and I'm not about to start now."

23

Cole

MACY'S UPSET, AND I don't blame her. It's been four hours since she froze at my side when I dismissed the question on air about the rumors between us and in that time, we haven't had a minute alone for me to explain. Or try to explain.

Not that there's anything I can say that can ease the sting I saw in her eyes, but I need to try.

On the surface, it would appear as if she's fine. No one else seems to have noticed the way she fidgeted with her bracelet in the car the entire way from the Rise & Shine studio down Broadway to where The Late Showdown tapes. No one else picked up on the fact she barely touched the salad she grabbed from the spread in the green room backstage when we had a few minutes for lunch. Even the makeup artist didn't mention Macy's brittle smile that's tearing me to pieces.

I should have answered the question. I should have quashed the rumors and replaced them with the truth. A truth I've known deep down since her voice echoed through the empty arena in Atlanta that December afternoon. A truth I felt in my soul the instant I laid eyes on her genuine smile. A truth that's been reinforced with every moment we've spent together, every chance I've gotten to know her, and especially when I learned how hard she's worked and how much she's sacrificed. How amazing she is.

I haven't tracked her down time and time again because she's just another *notch on my belt*, as she said. But it's easy to see why she might think so. The Cole she knows, the one I hope she still cares for, would never hurt her like that. Cole Heartwood, country star, on the other hand, did and is the asshole who's probably going to lose her for good.

From the side of the studio that serves as the stage, I catch Ben's eye and nod at Steven. Within seconds, they're both at my side. "Macy and I aren't going to do the photoshoot this afternoon. We're—"

"What?" Ben exclaims, gaping at me.

I hold up a hand to silence him and look at Steven. "After the interview, I want a car ready out back. Arrange for a horse-drawn carriage ride through Central Park, then shopping. FAO Schwarz first, then Bergdorf Goodman. We have dinner reservations at eight. After that, I want private access to the top of the Empire State Building and make sure my guitar is in the car. Call Tessa if you need help."

"Yes, sir."

"Cole—" Ben starts, a hopeful look in his eyes, but I cut him off by holding up a hand.

"This isn't what you think. It's just a way to make it up to Macy."

"You know how you can make it up to Macy," he says, cocking an eyebrow.

"Don't," I warn in a tone that invites no argument. I'm not ready to go public, and he and Melissa and the label just have to deal with that.

"Fine."

They move off, hopefully to make the arrangements, and I blow out a long breath. I wish Macy and I were already off, but it'll have to wait. We're about to perform our duet for the second time today, this time for a live studio audience.

I'm in place, looking for Macy, when a stagehand passes me my guitar. I slip my head through the strap and settle it against my hip when the crowd, which had finally quieted back down after I came out and said hello, breaks out in wild applause.

I spin, and my jaw drops. Macy wears a flowy cream-colored dress with a plunging neckline that almost reaches her navel. She lifts her arm to wave to the crowd, and the short dress raises so high I think the gentle curve of her ass is visible from behind. Plus, her legs in *those* boots look amazing.

Instead of glancing my way, Macy takes her place at her mic and reaches up to adjust her earpiece as a producer steps out from behind the cameras to doublecheck we're ready to record. With a thumbs up, the producer points to the host, who nods and waits for the countdown and red light to introduce us.

"And welcome back. I'm beyond thrilled that with us here tonight, celebrating the release of their new single, which hit number one and is sure to hold that spot for quite a while, please give it up for two-time male country music artist of the year, Cole Heartwood, and breakout star, Macy Porter!"

I play the opening notes and look up to meet Macy's eyes but wish I hadn't. She's turned to face me, but the smile on her lips doesn't reach her eyes. She gives the performance her all, as do I, but it's not the same. The spark that burned so brightly between us this morning is now more like a match than a bonfire.

Minutes later, the interview starts with the host praising our performance. I'm in the armchair next to his desk, while Macy is on the couch to my right, sitting a little too close for comfort to Asher Monroe, a pro quarterback whose thighs are as thick as tree trunks.

After a few questions about the song and the viral video that started it all, the host sets aside his cards. "Now, Macy, I have to ask, what's it like being the woman, who not only has a number one single in the country but also, rumor has it, has finally snared Cole Heartwood's heart?"

I hold my breath and turn to watch as Macy, without missing a beat, smiles and says, "Cole is a great guy, and I'm thrilled to have collaborated with him on this single, but the truth is, we're both focused on the music more than anything else, and our priorities are our careers."

I don't hear what the host says in response because I'm too busy reeling from the truth in her words. By not making our relationship public, I've proven I can't commit to anything or anyone and placed my career before her.

The steel in Macy's voice is like an arrow to my heart and carries the message that the same is now true for her. She's going to focus on the music and her career, and I don't blame her. I only hope it's not too late.

I'm distracted, cursing the fact I can't bring myself to confess my feelings and kiss her senseless right now in front of the cameras and the audience to prove she's more important to me than any of those things, but I'm snapped from my thoughts as the host nods toward Asher.

"Macy, looks like you've got options if you're single, after all. Asher, I see you have something to say?"

The quarterback shifts toward Macy and lays his arm across the back of the couch behind her, nearly touching the bare skin of her shoulder. "Yeah, any chance you're free after this?"

The audience erupts, and my fingers curl into fists as Macy smiles back at him and lifts a coy shoulder that brushes against his fingers. "Maybe."

24

Macy

"Change of plans? What do you mean change of plans?" I pull up short in the backstage hallway and rack my brain for what was last on our schedule for today. "Don't we have a photoshoot or something?"

"Not anymore." Cole growls out the words.

I meet his eyes, but he doesn't say more. Instead, he heaves a sigh and grabs my hand, leading me farther down a nondescript hallway toward an unmarked double door ahead with a red Exit sign above it.

My boots click on the laminate floor as I try to keep pace. Before we reach the door that leads to who knows where, I wriggle out of his grasp. "What is going on, Cole? We can't just leave."

"Yes, we can."

He's dead serious, but I cross my arms, determined not to budge until I get a straight answer. "Fine, if you want to leave so badly, why don't you tell me where you want to go and why you're slipping away without Ben and Melissa?"

He glances back down the hallway, bustling with activity, toward the studio before meeting my eyes. "I need you to trust me."

What?

I open my mouth, but before I can ask what the hell is going on, he steps toward me and presses a hand to the wall next to my head. "The shoot can be rescheduled. I...I have other plans for this afternoon. For you."

I narrow my gaze and whisper-hiss, "I am not skipping out on a photoshoot to sleep with you. Especially after this morning. I—"

"That's not what my plans are," he insists, his voice tight and a muscle working in his jaw.

I shake my head, trying to make sense of what is going on. "Cole, I—"

"Let's go before he tracks you down."

"He?"

Cole doesn't answer, but the pieces snap into place when he glances back down the hallway again.

"Do you mean Asher?"

Rather than answer, Cole grabs my hand. "Let's go."

So, this is what jealousy looks like on Cole Heartwood. I can't say it suits him, but I bite back a smile at this side of him I've never seen. A gruff, *you'll do what I say and like it* side I don't hate.

No man has ever been jealous of another on my account, and I'm finding it hard to believe for one second Cole would think I'm actually interested in Asher Monroe.

Sure, the pro quarterback is famous and fit, hot and rich, but he doesn't bring the soul Cole does. He can't sing a song just for me at midnight while we cuddle on my couch and talk for hours. He can't read me like a book and make me feel so wanted like Cole always has. He's never tracked me down until I didn't slip away anymore like Cole did.

Maybe, that's why Cole's answer to Ashley's question this morning was like a spear to my heart, piercing it until it bled out while I stood by silently and watched. I should have known better. Hell, I know how this industry works, and in that moment,

I realized no matter how close we've gotten, no matter how much I've let Cole into my life—into Mason's life—he's not the type of man to settle down. His priorities lie elsewhere, and I was a fool to ever believe I would be the woman to change him.

"No." I meet his eyes and give his hand a squeeze before I pull away. "I'm here for work. We both are. I can't just slip away with you. I have a reputation to repair, and we both have a job to do. You had your chance, and you blew it. If you want anything to do with me again, you need to get your shit together, because as far as I'm concerned, we're through."

And with that, I slip under his arm and out of reach, and he makes no move to stop me.

MELISSA SAID THE THEME for the magazine cover was high fashion, with a dash of royalty, and boy, she wasn't lying. By the time I'm done in hair and makeup, I barely recognize myself in the mirror. Not that false eyelashes, glossy lips and glittery eyeshadow will transform me on the inside, but looking like a million dollars does brighten my sour mood.

"Off to wardrobe," an assistant informs me as the makeup artist finishes up with a spritz of setting spray.

Melissa falls into step next to me as I follow the assistant down the hallway.

"Holding up okay?" she asks, giving me a sidelong glance, thanks, in part, I'm sure, to the stone-cold silence that filled the SUV all the way here.

During the ride, I tried to focus on the city streets outside the window instead of the man across the leather bench seat from me, but it was damn near impossible. At least, he came to his senses and joined us. I'm one thousand percent sure this shoot would have been canceled otherwise. No one was about to move forward with a magazine cover photo that only included me and not the heartthrob superstar they'd been counting on.

"Yeah, I'm fine."

"You sure? After that last segment—which was great, by the way," she adds, laying a manicured hand lightly on my arm, "It seems like you and Cole might be, I don't know... Having a falling out?"

A falling out? You can say that again.

I stop at the doorway to wardrobe and face her. "You have nothing to worry about. Cole and I are professionals, and we're here to do a job."

"Of course, yes, I know that," she says, waving away my assurance. "But I'm a professional, too, also here to do a job, and the sparks between you two, on and off the stage, are my business."

"It seems like you already know the answer to your question then, don't you? If today's interviews didn't make it clear to all of America that Cole and I aren't together, I'm not sure what you need from me."

"This afternoon, what I need from you are photos that paint a very different picture. One where the two of you are..."

She trails off as I glance past her, down the hallway, where an assistant emerges from another doorway with Steven and Ben on her heels. Then, a few steps behind, a man I know intimately but barely recognize comes into view.

Cole's head is down, his dark, unruly curls slicked back, but his muscular frame is unmistakable and striking in a black tuxedo that hugs every inch of him. He adjusts his cufflinks and rolls his neck as if he's uncomfortable, even though he looks like a million dollars.

My heart thumps, and I'm glad I'm not already dressed because I run my sweaty palms down my leggings. Cole might not want to claim me as his, but my body doesn't seem to care as he approaches, and every click of his shiny black dress shoes sends a flutter to the parts of me he knows exactly how to please.

I'm frozen, watching him as if time has slowed. He finally raises his gaze and sees me, his footsteps faltering as he slows. It might be my imagination, but the press of his lips into a tight line seems to ease just a touch, and his chin dips ever so slightly as he stops in front of us, the scent of his familiar cologne filling the air while his piercing gaze meets mine.

"We're not through, Macy. Not by a long shot."

My breath catches as he continues down the hallway, heading toward the set we were shown when we arrived, without waiting for a reply after dropping that bomb. I press a hand to my stomach as Melissa's eyes follow Cole for an instant and then narrow on me.

"Never mind," she says, with a smug, ruby-red smile. "I see I have nothing to worry about."

25

Cole

THE QUIET HUM OF the SUV's engine is doing nothing to soothe my nerves as we roll into downtown Kissing Springs. It's been forty-eight hours since Macy slipped away, *again,* in New York City. Almost two days since my knock on her hotel room door at The Plaza, that night after the photoshoot, went unanswered. Along with a text message and two phone calls since.

From what Steven tells me, she booked a last-minute seat on a commercial flight out of LaGuardia rather than waiting for the private jet we were scheduled to take together to pick up Mason here in Kentucky.

"She's just up ahead," Steven, who's behind the wheel, says, pulling me from my thoughts as he turns onto Main Street.

I glance at the screen on the dash, the red dot showing her location, our destination, now less than a block away, up ahead on the left.

"Pull over here."

He parks on the street, in a spot adjacent to a large town square with a white gazebo in the center, where a handful of kids are playing tag. Apparently, Macy is inside Hope's Diner. A place where the daily specials including chicken fried steak and blueberry pie are posted on an A-frame on the sidewalk out front.

"Wait," Steven says when I reach for the door handle. "Let me sweep the place first."

"No. I don't want her to spot you. You can keep eyes on me from here."

He glances around the square and in the side and rearview mirrors while I grab a baseball cap from the floorboard and slip it on. "I'll be inconspicuous. I promise." Especially because I need a minute to figure out exactly what I'm going to say.

A muscle works in his jaw, but Steven nods, and I slip out into the gloomy spring afternoon with a sky full of gray clouds threatening to burst at any minute. I pull my coat tighter around my shoulders and make my way down the street, keeping a close eye on the diner.

The last time I was here in Kissing Springs, on New Year's Day, seems like ages ago, though it's only been a few months. But in the time since then, things with Macy have changed so much. We were on a great trajectory until I went and fucked it all up.

Rather than cross at the intersection, I take a seat on a vacant worn wooden bench at the edge of the square. I've had hours to think about what I'd say when I saw her again, but now that I'm here, I'm second guessing everything. Macy keeps slipping away for good reasons, and my tactic of chasing after her each time isn't enough. Especially now, after I refused to confirm our status as a couple, even though deep down, a committed relationship with her is the one thing I want more than anything.

An elderly woman with leopard print pants shuffles by on the sidewalk. I meet her eyes and then, remembering my promise to Steven, glance away, tugging down my hat.

After she's passed, I study the diner, a quaint, one-story brick building situated between a post office and a hardware store. Lace curtains frame the windows, and I'd bet good money there's a counter inside with red vinyl stools bolted to the floor and a waitress who knows everyone's name. And would recognize an out-of-towner like me in an instant.

Movement in the glass catches my eye, and I freeze. Macy and Mason are in the booth next to the door, his little mop of dark curls barely visible in the window. Just then Macy laughs, her head thrown back and a wide smile on her face. A radiant, carefree, relaxed smile that's unlike any I've seen on her.

I'm glued to the scene, but my phone vibrates in my pocket, snapping me back to the present. Ben's name flashes on the screen. I debate not answering but lift it to my ear. "Yeah?"

"That good, huh?"

"Do you need something, or are you just calling to give me a hard time?"

"Have you seen the proofs from the photoshoot?"

"Did they come through?" My voice betrays my interest, and I grit my teeth at the sound of his lips curving into a smile on the other end of the line.

"Check your email. She looks amazing."

Immediately, I put him on speaker and pull up the email on my phone, clicking the link. Suddenly, there we are in the first image that loads. Me in a tux and Macy, every inch the gorgeous goddess, who eclipses me by a mile. From the instant she emerged from the dressing room in an exquisite golden gown, I only had eyes for her.

The dress, made from fabric that shimmered and sparkled in the light, hung gracefully from her every curve and stole my breath. It fell in a delicate swirl to the floor with a hidden slit that the stylist revealed in a striking pose captured in the first picture.

Macy's feet, in strappy gold stilettos, are planted in a confident stance, and she has one arm wrapped up around my neck while I stand behind her and stare down at her, my hand placed possessively on her hip.

"She's stunning," I murmur, unable to help myself. I scroll through the photos, and in every one, Macy's beauty and confidence radiates from her. Just as my adoration of her is unmistakable in every look on my face.

"Isn't she?" Ben agrees, chuckling softly. "I knew you two would look great together, but these photos... They're something else. You've got chemistry, Cole. It's undeniable, no matter what you both tell the world."

I swallow hard. Chemistry isn't the problem. It's my complete inability to commit to anything that stands in our way. And it's the reason I'm going to lose her.

When I don't respond, Ben pipes up again. "You there yet, man? In Kissing Springs?"

Damn Steven. I didn't specifically ask him not to tell anyone I was following Macy to Kentucky *again*, but I'd hope he'd keep it quiet. Apparently not.

"Uh, yeah," I say, lifting my gaze to find Macy and Mason through the diner window, once more. She's still smiling and reaches over to rumple Mason's hair. The small movement, so full of love and happiness, makes my heart ache. "Just arrived, but we'll be heading out in a minute."

"Leaving so soon?"

I blow out a long breath. "Yeah."

Silence falls and then, "We both know you've got a good heart, Cole. It's just buried beneath all that..."

"Bullshit?" I supply, managing a weak chuckle.

"I was going to say fear, but yeah, bullshit works, too."

"Fear?"

But he doesn't answer, doesn't clarify. He doesn't have to. The single word has struck a chord.

"You coming back to Nashville?" he asks, after another pause.

"No," I reply, realizing where I need to go to clear my head and get the dressing down I deserve. "I'm going to Alabama."

I don't need to say anything more. Ben knows me better than anyone, and he sure as hell knows exactly what's down south. Or rather, who.

"You need anything, you let me know, alright?"

"I will."

"I'll be here when you get back. After all, we've got another album to record."

I slip my phone into my coat pocket. Macy and Mason aren't in the booth anymore, and I scan the street, looking for them. The door to the post office opens, and the woman with the leopard print pants emerges just as Macy and Mason exit the diner, holding hands as they head down the sidewalk.

I want to call out her name, to watch her turn and recognize me here, in the town she loves, but I grip the bench with both hands instead. Macy wouldn't be thrilled to see me, right now, and I don't blame her. It wouldn't matter if I told her how much I miss her and want to be with her. For all my fame and fortune, I'm not the man she deserves—not yet, anyway.

Half a block down the street, they catch up to the gray-haired woman just outside the door of the Kissing Springs Public Library and hold it open for her before following her inside. I remember something about Hannah being a librarian, here in town, and wonder if they're stopping by to visit her.

I stare at the door for what seems like an eternity, then with one final long exhale, I rise and retrace my steps back to the SUV.

Steven is silent when I climb in and buckle up.

"To the airport," I tell him.

Without a word, he shifts into park while I pull out my phone and text Tessa.

I'm going to visit my grandfather in Monroe County, Alabama for a few days

Have whatever I'll need delivered, including my guitar

Her response comes through immediately.

Yes, sir

And send flowers to Macy when she gets back to Nashville

What would you like the note to read?

I stare at the question. I should say something, but at the moment, there's nothing that will make any of this better.

Nothing. Leave it blank

I toss my phone in the cupholder, lean back, and stare out the window, rubbing my temple. As we drive away from Kissing Springs, the sun, still hidden behind the clouds, dips lower in the sky, casting shadows as dusk settles over the quaint buildings and tree-lined streets. But the sights barely register.

I'm leaving my heart behind, here in Kissing Springs, but the man I was three months ago, the man I still am now isn't enough. Ben's right, I've got changes to make to become someone Macy deserves, a man who can give her and Mason the unconditional love they deserve. It's that or lose her forever, and there's no way in hell I'll let that happen.

July | Kissing Springs

You love me and its inviting,
to go where life is more exciting
But I was raised on country sunshine
~ Country Sunshine by Dottie West

26

Macy

Emerging from the cool, quiet refuge of my trailer in the lot behind the amphitheater, the sweltering summer heat hits me like a wall. I hold the bar by the door and carefully step down to the trampled grass in my short skirt and now famous cowgirl boots. The smell of sunscreen, sweat, and beer clings to the humid air, mixing with excitement that buzzes from the crowd on the other side of the stage.

Cheers erupt from the audience of thousands spread over the great lawn, less than fifty yards away, as another artist's set ends. The impressive structure, which I was thrilled to be invited to perform at, was built within the last two years for exactly the type of large-scale outdoor music festival Kissing Springs has welcomed this weekend.

I take a deep breath and follow a stagehand wearing a fanny pack and a headset, who weaves through the trailers and buses parked back here for the dozen country music artists in the festival's lineup. A roster that doesn't include Cole Heartwood.

I push aside the thought as I have whenever *he's* popped into my mind over the last four months. Since New York City, it's been nothing but radio silence from Cole, not that we haven't been linked frequently, thanks to the single and continued speculation about our relationship. But right now, I have a performance to focus on and no time for the ever-present ache in my chest.

Anticipation runs through my veins, as it always does, before I step onstage for a live audience, especially one this big. I don't think it's something I'll ever get used to—or tired of. But as we turn a corner and pass a security guard stationed under a canopy, I catch a familiar sight out of the corner of my eye.

"Is that...?" I mumble, pulling up short to study the sleek, jet-black tour bus with tinted windows and a familiar image on the door. A small white Wanderlust logo. That same call back to Heartwood's breakthrough debut album I laid eyes on eight months ago.

My heart skips a beat as completely unexpected recognition dawns. It's Cole's bus.

"Wait, is he here?" I ask the stagehand, my palms growing clammy and my stomach twisting into a knot.

"Who?" Her eyes flick to follow my line of vision.

"Cole Heartwood."

"I don't know," she says with a shrug, taking another step up the stairs. "But I've got to get you backstage. Jackson's already there and the sound tech is wondering where you are."

I nod but don't move while my mind races. *Why is his bus here? Why would he be here? Why now? He's not on the schedule.*

Cole, the country music superstar I'd foolishly fallen for, the man I was drawn to like a magnet, our chemistry undeniable, finally gave up on me. He's kept his distance, and I thought he'd never track me down again. But this glimpse, knowing he's here, is jarring. It doesn't make sense.

"Hey, Macy, you ready?" the stagehand asks, jolting me from my reverie.

"Uh, yeah." I tear my gaze away from Cole's bus. "I'm ready."

"Great, you're up in five," she says, taking the stairs two at a time.

"Five minutes." I repeat those two simple words, willing my racing thoughts into submission. But the image of Cole's bus plagues me, each second that ticks by bringing a fresh wave of confusion.

But, summoning every ounce of resolve I possess, I take a deep breath and follow her, slipping behind the curtain as the announcer comes on the speakers. "Next up, ladies and gentlemen, in less than five minutes, none other than hometown favorite, Macy Porter!"

The thunderous roar of the crowd reverberates through my core. Cole may be nearby, but right now, it's just me and my music performing for this crowd. Whatever comes next can wait until the final note has faded.

THE SUN BLAZES DOWN from a clear blue summer sky over the Kissing Springs Music Festival, casting its golden rays over the sea of cowboy hats and tank tops in the thick crowd as I step out on stage. The heat is oppressive, and sweat instantly forms on my brow, but the adrenaline coursing through my veins makes me feel alive.

I shoot the crowd a wide smile and grab the microphone as the opening notes of a song from my first album starts to play. It's a personal favorite that's become popular now that I have.

I give the audience everything, pouring my heart into every word I sing.

"Thank you, Kissing Springs!" I shout into the microphone, basking in the applause that washes over me when the song ends.

Finally, it's time for the last song in my set.

"Alright, folks," I say, trying to sound breezy and unaffected by the turmoil within. "I've got a special duet planned for y'all today. Please welcome...Jackson Reynolds!"

I hold out my arm for the up-and-coming male country artist I've sung the duet with a few times now to join me onstage. The label brought in the musician with a baritone again today, a decision made weeks ago, when Cole's lack of attendance at this festival was confirmed.

Jackson emerges from the wings in his familiar black gambler cowboy hat and waves to the crowd, shooting me a warm smile as we exchange a quick nod before launching into the first verse. Our voices are technically a perfect blend, but it's not the same as it was with Cole. It never is.

But as we reach the bridge, something unexpected happens. Jackson steps back and interrupts the song to say, "Thank you, Kissing Springs," waving to the crowd as if he's leaving.

My jaw drops, but I scramble to continue the next verse as the music plays on. Then, out of nowhere, another voice joins mine, an unmistakable rich, velvety timbre.

Cole, his eyes locked on mine, steps onstage. A collective gasp ripples through the audience, followed by deafening cheers when they realize what's happening. My heart hammers wildly against my ribcage, a mixture of elation and disbelief threatening to overwhelm me. But somehow, I manage to find my voice, joining him in perfect harmony.

"Maybe, it's time we face the truth," I sing, our voices rising together in a crescendo that sends shivers down my spine.

"Maybe, it's time we stop runnin'," Cole sings, his gaze never leaving mine.

With each word, the distance between us shrinks, the magnetic pull of our connection growing stronger by the second. The energy between us crackles like lightning, and for a moment, it feels as if nothing else exists but the two of us on this stage.

"Hey there, sweetheart'," he murmurs, leaning in close, so only I can hear him during an interlude. "Mind if I join you?"

I have no words. My mouth is dry. I'm still reeling from his appearance and trying to make sense of what's happening and the fact his presence is sending sparks through my entire body.

He reaches for my hand, and I grasp his tight, holding on for dear life as the notes play on. His expression softens into a tentative smile. There's a hint of vulnerability in his eyes I've never seen, but it's mixed with the firm look of resolve that's exactly the Cole I remember.

When it's time to sing again, my tongue darts out to wet my lips, and we launch back into the song, our voices blending seamlessly as if we've never been apart.

"Thank you, Kissing Springs!" Cole yells as the last note fades away. The audience erupts into applause once more, and their cheers drown out the pounding of my heart.

I'm breathless, my emotions tangled and raw, but I join him in waving to the crowd. "Thank you, Kissing Springs!"

When I look over at Cole, his eyes lock with mine for a split second before he turns away and swiftly exits the stage.

"What a performance by Macy Porter with Jackson Reynolds and extra special surprise guest, Cole Heartwood!" The festival MC joins me onstage as I stare at the curtain Cole's disappeared through, leaving me standing there, dumbstruck and aching for answers.

"What a performance, Macy," the MC says with a warm smile, "Thanks again for being here with us for the Kissing Springs Summer Music Festival!"

My mind whirls as I try to hold it together and take a bow, rushing offstage the instant I can, my breath coming fast and hard.

"Hey, have any of you seen Cole?" I ask the group behind the curtain getting ready to take the stage. They shake their heads and seem just as surprised by Cole Heartwood's sudden appearance as I am.

"Sorry, Macy," one of them offers. "But if we see him, we'll send him your way."

"Thanks," I reply, my voice barely audible above the noise of the festival.

I weave through the crowded backstage area, looking for any sign of Cole, but he seems to have vanished.

"Damn it, Cole," I mutter under my breath, unable to keep the frustration from seeping into my veins. How could he show up, surprise me on stage, and then slip away? Is he trying to give me a taste of my own medicine?

Something tells me, no, but also, that I haven't seen the last of him this weekend.

27

Cole

A FAMILIAR BARK INSIDE announces my arrival as I take the steps two at a time up to Hannah and Hunter's front porch and lift a hand to offer a friendly wave at the elderly neighbor watching me from next door. Daisy rounds the corner from the kitchen and barrels toward the front door, a blur of black-and-white spotted fur announcing a visitor.

Through the open screen door, I see Hannah following before I even ring the bell. Daisy bounds back, nails clicking on the wooden floorboards as Hannah, with a half-smile, welcomes me inside. "Right on time."

"I'm a man of my word."

She hesitates for barely an instant, but it's long enough I notice and swallow hard. I've still got work to do, but that's why I'm here. I'm ready.

"That was quite the surprise," she says, absently petting Daisy.

Hannah had said she'd head over to the festival for Macy's performance, and I'm glad she was there to see it.

"Not as much of a surprise as I'd hoped, but not bad."

"What do you mean?"

"Macy saw my bus in the back lot." It was over an hour ago, but the sensation that ran through every inch of me when the recognition dawned in her eyes remains. When her feet had tripped up and she'd frozen, confusion written all over her face while she stared.

She couldn't see me through the tinted windows, couldn't be sure I watched her, but I was, and I did until she was out of sight backstage. It took every ounce of patience, and my grandpa's voice in my head, not to open the door, step out right then, and apologize for everything.

And I'm glad I didn't because I've got a plan, and I pray it's enough.

"But the chemistry is still there, don't you think?" Hannah asks.

The look on Macy's face when I stepped on that stage was a blend of surprise and confusion with a flash of longing, and in that moment, I knew in my heart I still had a chance. I meet Hannah's eyes, so much like Macy's baby blues. "I do."

"When you reached out to me, I had my doubts, but after seeing you two together onstage, it seems I made the right call."

"Thanks for everything." I glance around the old home, Grandma Porter's house, as Macy still refers to it as. A home I walked away from on New Year's morning, unsure I'd ever be back.

"Of course." Her eyes narrow. "You still sure about this? About Macy?"

I duck my head and rub the back of my neck. She asked me the same thing when I called out of the blue weeks ago to ask for her help. "Without a doubt."

"Good." She nods as if it's a done deal, and I wish it was that easy and already decided. But convincing Macy I've changed, that I'd do anything for her, will not be as easy. Although the look in her eyes, the electricity still between us onstage gives me hope I'm on the right path.

"Ready for tonight?"

Heat crawls up my spine when I think about seeing Macy again—really seeing her. "As I'll ever be."

"I haven't told Mason you're going to watch him for a few hours, but I'm sure he'll be thrilled. He's out back just now. Tanner dropped him off a few minutes ago." She turns to head toward the back door. "I'll go grab him."

"Thanks, Hannah." Nerves and anticipation tangle in my gut. It's been months since I last saw the little guy, but if I know Mason, it'll be as if we were never apart.

A screen door slams, followed by the patter of little feet. "Mr. Heartwood!"

I ignore the formality he's slipped back into after my disappearance and drop to my knees. "Hey, buddy."

"Is it true?" he asks, a skeptical look on his little face.

"Is what true?"

"That I get to play with you for a few hours?"

He inches closer, and I breathe in his little boy scent—dirt and sunshine and something sweet like bubble gum.

I ruffle his hair, unable to keep from smiling. "It's true. Whaddya say we go on an adventure?"

Mason whoops, pumping a fist in the air. My heart swells, overflowing with affection for this kid who's taken my extended absence in stride.

"What sounds like fun?" I ask, rising and addressing Hannah as much as Mason.

Mason considers me for a long moment before his expression clears. "The springs!" He grabs my hand, already tugging me toward the driveway. "We can 'xplore and skip rocks and watch for fish and... Bye, Hannah. See you later!"

"Bye buddy! Have fun!" With a wave, Hannah sends us off, but not before I meet her eyes.

"I'll drop him back off by five and then see you tonight?"

She nods. "We'll be there."

Mason grins up at me, ignoring anything that sounds like boring adult talk. "Have you ever skipped rocks, Mr. Heartwood?"

"Not in a long, long time."

MASON IS CROUCHED BY the bubbling creek, intently searching the rocky bank.

"What are you looking for?" I ask.

"The perfect rock," he answers, not glancing up.

"Ah, I see." I squat beside him and run my fingers through the cool water. "My grandpa taught me how to pick the right rock. You want one that's smooth and flat, not too big or too small. One that fits comfortably in your hand, with an edge that cuts through the water just right."

I pick up one that could fit the bill and hand it to him. He looks up at me. "Your grandpa taught you?" At my nod, he asks, "Did you skip rocks a lot when you were little?"

"All the time." I pick up another rock, testing its weight and shape in my hand before rising and sending it skipping across the creek with a splash. "I'd spend hours down by the creek, hunting for rocks and frogs and whatever else I could find. I was maybe your age or a little older, at the time."

"I'm almost six."

"You have a birthday coming up?" Some quick mental math based on what I know of Mason's conception puts his birthday in August or maybe early September.

He nods enthusiastically, his dark curls shining in the dappled sun's rays making their way through the thick oak trees. "Yep! I'm gonna be six!"

"Six, huh? Wow, so big. Any special birthday plans?"

"We're going to the zoo!" Mason skips another rock, making it farther this time. He peers up at me with those bright blue eyes. "You'll come, won't you, Cole?" His high voice is so full of hope and expectation, my heart melts. Plus, he called me Cole.

I kneel so we're eye-to-eye, resting my hands on his shoulders. "Wild horses couldn't keep me away, buddy. I'll be there to celebrate with you, I promise."

"Yay!" Mason throws his arms around my neck, hugging me tight. "This is gonna be the best birthday ever!"

I close my eyes and breathe in the moment, wrapping my arms around his slight frame and hoping to hell his mom doesn't take exception to my promise.

As we wander along the bank farther away from the springs, I can't help but enjoy the warm summer day. My mind wanders to where it has been nonstop since March. To Macy.

She never asked for much. Hell, if anything, she made it clear she didn't want special treatment. All she ever wanted was what any woman deserves. For her man to put her first. I didn't, and it's taken a long time and a lot of therapy to get here. My grandpa was the one to sum it up. *When music was there for you more than your mom, it's no wonder that guitar's the only thing you've committed to.*

But I'm ready now. Ready to give Macy my all, if she'll have me, and never look back.

Steven, who's been hovering in the background, approaches and clears his throat. I take a deep breath and blow it out, watching Mason for one more minute. I'm grateful for the time with him today, no matter what happens tonight. I pick up two rocks and hand one to him. "Last one, little man."

He sends his sailing, then I let mine fly. It catches the surface just right and goes farther than any attempt so far.

"Wow, you're like a pro," Mason says, giving me a high five.

"Thanks, but it's time to head back now, buddy. Your mom was busy with press and interviews, but she'll be done soon."

Mason sighs but takes my hand. "Today was fun. Can we do it again, sometime? Maybe at home?"

I give his hand a squeeze. He means Nashville, although I know Macy would love to make Kissing Springs his home and raise him here. "Absolutely."

We climb into the back of the SUV, and Mason spends the ride back running Hot Wheels over his legs and around the leather bench while I gaze out the window at the passing scenery. The picturesque, lush, rolling fields and wide-open spaces are something I could get used to. This is a place where I could put down the roots I've been avoiding for way too long. If Macy will have me, that is.

28

Macy

IT DOESN'T MATTER THAT we lost Grandma Porter years ago. To this day, every time I step inside what's now Hannah's old craftsman-style house, I still smell my grandma's perfume, a sweet fragrant blend of fresh roses and lilies that lingers. The delicate smell fit her gentle temperament but was strong enough to match her backbone. It's familiar and comforting and wraps around me like a warm blanket, which is just what I need after the whirlwind day I've had at the festival.

"Hey," I call out as the screen door closes behind me and my boots click on the hardwood floor.

"In here." Hannah's reply comes from the den. I head in there to find her and Mason sitting crisscross applesauce on the floor in front of the coffee table. They're in the middle of a game of Candyland while the late-afternoon sun filters through the lace curtains, casting dappled shadows on the wall.

"Hey, bud, how was your day?" I press a kiss to the top of his head and sink onto the couch, taking another swig from the water bottle I carried in.

Hunter, a Kissing Springs firefighter, had to work the festival today, although I didn't see him there, so Hunter's brother, Tanner, agreed to watch Mason for a few hours while Hannah joined Chloe and Lucas for my portion of the show.

"Mommy!" he exclaims, looking up from the game. "I skipped rocks with Cole at the springs!"

I smile at the pure joy on his face, but my heart skips a beat when I process his words. Then it comes to a screeching halt. *Cole?*

Cole, Cole?

My eyes shoot to Hannah, but I temper my voice as I say, "You did?"

"Yup, and he's going to come to my birthday party and take me rock skipping again at home and—"

"Wait, what?" I shake my head, but the confusion doesn't dissipate. After surprising me at the show, Cole came here and took Mason to the springs? And made promises he can't keep?

None of this makes sense. Starting with how Cole convinced Hannah to let him take my son for a few hours without my consent.

"Hey, Mason," Hannah says, seemingly prepared for the conversation to come. "Why don't you see if your tablet is charged and go upstairs and play for a few minutes while I talk to your mommy, okay?"

Mason doesn't need to hear the word tablet twice. He has unplugged his device and is scampering up the stairs with Daisy on his heels before we can change our minds.

"Macy," Hannah starts, her voice low as she lifts herself up onto the couch to face me. "It was just for a couple of hours. They had fun."

"Where is he now?" I demand, scanning the room, half-expecting Cole to step out from the kitchen, that gorgeous grin on his face, to surprise me again. But he's not here.

"He dropped off Mason and left about twenty minutes ago."

"Oh." The hurt lingers in my voice, even though I try to mask it. As much as I want to be angry, part of me is disappointed he's not here, waiting to see me again, but my mind still spins. "What? So he just shows up and asks to see Mason and you're like, *'okay, sure, no problem',* even though the man has been radio silent for months?"

My voice creeps higher as my tirade continues through gritted teeth.

"Damn it, Hannah," I mutter, running a hand through my hair. "Really? Cole, of all people?"

"You're the one who told him to stay away, Macy. To *get his shit together*, from what I understand."

"Exactly. So just because he reappears and asks nicely you think, *'okay sure, take Macy's son for a few hours, no problem?'*"

Hannah doesn't bite but simply raises her eyebrows and gives me a look I know well. A look that reminds me of my grandmother. After a long moment, she reaches out and rests her hand on my arm. "We've both seen the headlines. You can't deny he's made every effort to do exactly as you asked."

"Headlines don't tell the whole story." My voice is soft as I stare down at my hands. "I need more than tabloid gossip to convince me he's really changed. Plus, he's not the one who's been in the public eye the last few months. He hasn't had to face the same question time and time again about what's going on between the two of us."

Hannah nods, her gaze steady and understanding. "You've handled everything so well, but Cole's shown genuine commitment lately. Aren't you the one who mentioned he signed a three-record deal with his label? And the profile online was all about how he's started a foundation to support children living in poverty with access to the arts."

I'm glad she doesn't add the fact he's gone solo to two high-profile events recently and hasn't been spotted with a woman—any woman—since me in New York.

Her words hang in the air, heavy with their implications. I bite my lip, struggling to maintain the wall I've built around my heart. I told Cole to go, but he's been silent for so long I've been left to wonder if he ever truly cared. Now, faced with evidence of his growth, I'm torn between anger over his silence and hope that he might have changed after all.

"Commitment to his career is one thing, Hannah," I say, forcing myself to focus on the facts. "But that doesn't mean he's ready for a relationship—especially one with a single mom and all the responsibilities that come with that."

"True," she concedes, her expression thoughtful. "But isn't it possible he's committing to things that matter, even if it's not in the way you might expect?"

I cross my arms over my chest, trying to keep the hurt at bay. "I can't believe you're taking his side."

"I'm not taking sides, but it's impossible not to notice how much you two are drawn to each other, even after all this time. I mean, look at what happened on stage only a few hours ago!"

"Drawn to each other?" I scoff, looking off out the window. "That's not enough, Hannah. Not for me. Not for a real relationship." The lump in my throat grows thick, making it hard to swallow.

"Okay, but let me ask you this," she presses, her voice gentle but insistent. "How did you feel when Cole surprised you on stage? Be honest, Macy."

I bite my lip, unwilling to admit the truth, that the moment our eyes met, I was transported back to a time when we were inseparable, when the chemistry between us was undeniable. "It...it was good," I whisper finally, my eyes meeting hers.

"See?" she says triumphantly, a knowing smile gracing her lips. "You owe it to yourself to at least give Cole a chance to prove himself."

"Believe me, I want to," I admit, my heart aching with longing. "If he wants to see me so badly, why didn't he wait here? Why did he slip away again?" But as I say the words an echo of our conversation from months ago flickers through my mind. When Cole told me he'd gotten a taste of what it felt like when I walked away, when I slipped off without saying goodbye.

Now, I see exactly what he meant. I close my eyes and take a deep breath, filling my lungs as I wrestle with my conflicting emotions.

"Give him a chance, Macy," she pleads, squeezing my arm. "He cares about you and Mason. I can tell. I wouldn't have let him near your son if I didn't believe it, and you know it."

I bite my lip and look away, unable to meet her gaze. It's true. The recent news stories about Cole paint a very different picture from the rockstar playboy who earned his reputation. But he's chosen to stay away, so it's still so hard to know if he's even capable of the commitment I need.

A sigh escapes me as the weight of her words hangs in the summer air. The truth is, part of me wants to believe Cole has changed, that he's ready to commit and be the man I want him to be. But the rest of me is terrified of getting hurt again. After all, these past few months, while great career-wise, have been tainted because he wasn't there to share them with.

"So, do you think he's that much different now than he was in March?" My chest tightens when I say the words and realize they might actually be true.

Hannah lifts a shoulder. "I'm just saying people change. And from what I've seen, Cole's trying to prove to you he has."

"Maybe," I whisper, allowing myself just a sliver of hope. "But actions speak louder than words, Hannah. He needs to prove he's serious about *us*, not just his career, but his personal life, too."

"Fair enough," she says, her voice gentle but firm. "Just promise me you'll keep an open mind, alright? You deserve happiness, Macy. And maybe, just maybe, Cole is the one who can give it to you."

"Fine," I say finally, my voice cracking with emotion. "But if Cole wants to be part of our lives, he needs to prove he's here to stay."

Hannah nods, her eyes filled with understanding. "I think that's fair. And I truly believe Cole wants to make things right this time." A secretive smile crosses her face, and I swear there's a twinkle in her eye. "Maybe, sooner than you think."

"Wait, what?" I demand, my pulse racing. "What do you know that I don't?"

"Nothing."

I can tell she's lying because she's terrible at it, always has been. Her bottom lip tucks between her teeth, and she fidgets, looking off and not meeting my eyes.

Pushing Hannah for answers will be futile, though. She can keep a secret better than a biometric high-security vault. But she said I may find out something sooner than I think, so apparently, I just need to be patient. If only it were that easy.

29

Cole

If you'd have asked me on New Year's Eve if I'd ever step foot inside The Bourbon Boot Scoot again, I would have guessed not, but here I am, pacing back and forth, my boots clicking on the empty hardwood dance floor while I breathe in the old wood, whiskey, and cigarette smoke, now tinged with a fragrant bouquet.

The long, bottle-lined bar is still there, as is the small stage and DJ booth at the back, but otherwise, the place has been transformed.

"Is everything to your satisfaction, Mr. Heartwood?" Tessa's voice comes through my earbud from my phone.

I glance around again. "Yes, it's...perfect."

Really. Tessa outdid herself this time. With barely three weeks' notice, my PA pulled together all the details, starting with convincing the bar owner to rent out the place for the night, which probably wasn't easy or cheap with the crowds in town for the festival. But it doesn't matter. Whatever the price, I'm happy to pay.

And that was just the beginning. Tessa also went above and beyond to create the perfect atmosphere. Twinkling lights wrap around every wooden beam and are strung from the ceiling, casting a warm glow on the rustic walls. Delicate bouquets of wildflowers grace each table, and the stage is adorned with white rose petals on the floor, surrounding the single stool and my old guitar waiting on its stand.

"Ms. Carmel, from *The Country Music Chronicle*, is outside awaiting your sign."

I move to the window and glance out. As expected, Steven is in the SUV across the street, keeping eyes on the place. No doubt, he's got additional security out back, too.

Tony, the same guard who was on duty on New Year's Eve, blocks the door, turning away would-be patrons and brushing off their disappointment to hear the bar is closed for the night for a private party.

A few feet away, Ms. Carmel, the reporter Tessa arranged to be here, thanks to the promise of a chance to break a headline, waits, as expected, with a laptop bag slung over her shoulder.

"Is there anything else I can do for you, sir?"

"Wish me luck," I reply, only half-joking as my heart pounds while I try not to think about what I'll do if Macy says no.

"Good luck, Cole. I can't wait to hear how it goes. I'm here if you need anything at all."

"Thanks, Tessa." I press End and slide my earbud into my left pocket and touch my hand to the right, as if to reassure myself the ring in the box is still there, that I haven't lost it.

My heart leaps into my throat as I see Hannah pull over on the street in an old Buick, with Macy sitting shotgun. After a brief conversation, Macy emerges from the car, looking absolutely stunning in a sexy dress that hugs her curves.

Her high heels remind me of the ones she wore on New Year's, here in this bar, and the similar pair she had on for the photoshoot in New York City. Her mile-long legs are sexy as hell, and I swallow hard, watching her glance around.

With a half wave to Hannah, Macy turns her attention to the bar, her brows furrowing. There's no doubt she knows I'm in here, and my chest tightens when she stands there, unmoving. As if she's unsure whether to enter or run. Before she can make up her mind, a handful of fans surround her, seeking selfies and autographs and generally getting too close for comfort.

My hands curl into fists at my side, and I'm one second away from throwing the door open when Tony catches sight of what's going on and shoves his way through the horde to guide Macy to the door.

I step back from the window, prepared to face the most important moment of my life, and send one last prayer heavenward. I've worked hard to overcome my issues, but now that she's here, the time has come to lay it all on the line, and doubt rears its ugly head.

The door creaks open, and I hold my breath as Macy slips inside. Her eyes widen when she scans the transformed space. The twinkling lights cast a warm glow over her face, making her look even more beautiful. She hesitates for a moment, clearly not having expected this, and I can't help it. I take a step toward her and softly say her name.

She tears her eyes away from the stage to meet mine, the weight of her gaze almost tangible.

"I had a feeling I'd see you again soon." Her tone is low and flat, as if she can't quite decide how she feels about all this.

"I'm sorry, Macy. I was a fool not to jump at the chance to call you mine when it stared me in the face. I'm sorry for not shouting from the rooftops how you made me the happiest man alive and I couldn't live without you. I was a fool, and...I'm sorry."

Her eyebrows shoot to the ceiling, and I can tell a profuse apology was not what she expected. Hell, it wasn't how I thought this would start, although every word I said was true and needed to be spoken.

"Look," I say, running my fingers through my hair. "You don't have to say anything, but I wrote a song for you. Will you listen?"

"I thought you weren't a songwriter?"

"Seems like, maybe, I am when it's the only way to say how I feel."

Her eyes flick to the stage and back to mine. "Okay."

It's a good start. She hasn't turned and let the door slam closed behind her on the way out yet.

I make my way to the stage and take a deep breath, relishing the comfort my old guitar has always provided. I prop myself on the stool, resting one boot on the rung while the other remains on the floor. Slowly, I strum the familiar chords of the song I've workshopped a thousand times over the past few months. I've sung the song so many times my grandpa told me if I didn't get outta town and sing it for Macy, he'd do it himself.

That was three weeks ago today.

My heart pounds as the first verse spills from my lips. While I sing, Macy's expression shifts from curiosity to understanding and then to pure emotion.

It's everything I've wanted to tell her and more.

As the last note echoes through the bar, her eyes shimmer with unshed tears, and the whisper of hope snaking through me grows.

"Did you really write that for me, Cole?" Her voice, rather than low and flat, is now choked with emotion.

"Every word. And I mean it. Macy, I'm ready to give you my all, to commit to you and our future together. I just... I need you to know how much you mean to me."

Her eyes glisten as she takes a step closer to the stage, her hands trembling at her sides. "I want to believe you, Cole. I really do. But how is this time different? What's changed?"

They're fair questions, yet they stab at my heart. I hurt her when I refused to confirm we were together, but I've grown since then. And I'm desperate to prove it to her.

I set aside my guitar and step down, taking hold of both of her hands.

"You told me to leave and for good reason. I didn't deserve to be your man then. But these past few months, I've taken the time, like you said, and figured things out."

I step closer as if willing her to understand and believe. "You and Mason are the most important people in my life. You make me whole, and the last thing I want is for you to slip away again."

She presses her lips together while I continue, my gaze locked on hers. "But there's something else you should know. Outside, right now, there's a national reporter waiting to interview you. She's here so I can set the record straight because I was a fool not to profess my love for you to the world before, but I'm more than ready now, if you are."

Her eyes narrow and search mine. "You're really ready to go public with our relationship, Cole? Are you sure?"

"I am. I want everyone to know I'm the lucky one who finally convinced Macy Porter to love him, flaws and all."

"No one will believe it," she says, brushing off my words as she squeezes my fingers. "I'll still be *the one who finally won Cole Heartwood's heart*."

My throat constricts. "Is that a yes? A yes that you'll be mine and I can tell the world how lucky I am?"

Her blue eyes twinkle in the white lights, filled with a mix of emotions—hope and fear, joy and uncertainty—while a soft, hesitant smile plays on her lips. I'm asking her to take a leap of faith and trust me, and I don't blame her for thinking about it.

But this is the moment when everything could change, and so, with a deep breath, I inch even closer, and this time, she follows suit, the warmth of her body pressing against mine.

30

MACY

SO MANY EMOTIONS ROLL through me it feels as if I have whiplash, but the place my heart settles on is...love. Because it's clear. This man standing in front of me is not the same one I said goodbye to months ago in New York City. And I can't forget that Cole doesn't say things that aren't true.

"Yes," I whisper, looking up at the man whose dark eyes betray his apprehension. "You can tell the world I'm yours, Cole Heartwood, because I have been since that first night."

His shoulders fall, and he breaks into that famous smile and presses a quick kiss to my lips, which I try to lean in to but can't. Rather than wrap me up in his arms, Cole drops to one knee, his eyes pinned to mine. It's as if the wind is knocked out of me when he pulls a box from his pocket and opens it to reveal a dazzling diamond solitaire.

"Macy," he begins, his voice steadier now. "You are the love of my life. You've changed me for the better, and I want nothing more than to spend the rest of my life proving my love to you." A pause and then, "Will you marry me?"

My jaw drops, and I take a step back then another. My hand flies to my chest as thoughts whirl through my mind like a tornado.

"Marry?" I whisper, staring down at the flawless emerald-cut precious gem as my head shakes back and forth. "I…I thought we were making progress by announcing our relationship. We…we can't go from zero to a hundred in two-point-two seconds. I—"

"Why not?" he asks, sliding toward me and reaching for my hand. "From that first night, Macy, you had my heart, even if I didn't want to admit it. I couldn't stay away then, and even now, wild horses couldn't keep me from you. I believe you feel the same, and I know it's going to take time, but please, sweetheart, say you'll be my wife."

Tears fill my eyes, and one slips down my cheek. I brush it away as his words settle. "Okay," I say with a lift of my shoulders as I smile and realize I want nothing more than to have this persistent, talented, thoughtful man by my side every day for the rest of my life. "I'll marry you."

"Really?" His tone betrays his disbelief.

"Really," I confirm with a laugh as he rises and pulls me into his arms, lifting me off my feet and kissing me soundly, with a kiss that tastes like joy and love and forever. "But only if I get to meet the man who set you straight."

"My grandpa?"

"Isn't that where you've been? Down in a small town in Alabama where your grandpa lives?"

"It is, and you're right. He did set me straight, and he's dying to meet you. I'm sure he'll love you as much as I do."

"I can't wait."

As he sets me down, he eyes the window by the front door, and I remember the reporter from *The Country Music Chronicle* waiting outside, ready to break the official story of Cole Heartwood's *relationship*—or now engagement, I suppose.

"Hey." He presses a lingering kiss to my lips. "What do you say we postpone that interview until tomorrow? We have some celebrating to do."

"Sounds perfect. Let's focus on us tonight."

"Us," he echoes, wrapping his arms around my waist as his nose wrinkles. "And all of your Kissing Springs friends and family."

"What?" I glance around to look for them as if they're here, ready to pop out and surprise me. I thought we were alone, that this moment was private, but maybe, I was wrong.

The bar is completely empty. The pieces fall into place in my mind, and I eye Cole. "Hannah Porter wouldn't happen to have anything to do with this, would she?"

He shrugs. "I'm very convincing when I've made up my mind."

You can say that again. I shake my head and roll my eyes but lift on my toes for another kiss. "Tell me about it."

THE AIR CONDITIONING BLASTS, sending a chill down my sweat-soaked skin as I stumble up the steps and onto the tour bus, still parked behind the concert venue. My head spins from the drinks at the bar, starting with a champagne toast and ending with a shot of good ole Lockland Kentucky bourbon with Hannah, Chloe, and Lucas, but that doesn't stop the heat pooling low in my belly as Cole's smoky gaze rakes over me, his lips curving into a sultry smile as his fingers weave through mine.

He's been by my side all night, ever since he slipped the diamond ring on my finger. I look down at it now, and my heart flutters, but at the moment, the undeniable ache for his touch rules over any coherent thought I can manage.

The gentle hum of the generator fills the bus like a lullaby as I reach for the counter to steady myself while I glance around the interior I haven't seen since that first night. It seems like forever ago now, and so much has changed since December, but one thing that hasn't is the heat between us, the chemistry, the magnetism.

I wrap my arms around Cole's neck and kiss him, nibbling and licking my way along his lower lip while his fingers grip my waist, staking their claim. Cologne mixed with sweat and arousal fills the air and sends shivers down my spine.

He shuffles us, still pressed together, down the hallway, bumping into the wall and earning him a giggle before we finally make it to the bedroom, where he releases me to kick shut the door and whip his shirt off over his head.

"Jeans, too," I say, detecting the slur in my words as I kick off my heels and tug at the hem of my dress, which clings to my damp skin.

"Yes, ma'am," he replies, in a thick Southern drawl that's more pronounced, thanks to his recent extended stay in southern Alabama and however many drinks he had at the bar.

Naked and fully erect, Cole slides onto the bed and, propped up, tugs me onto his lap. I'm still wearing my bra and panties, and his large hands grip my waist as I straddle him, our bodies pressing together in all the right places. I shimmy against his cock and reach behind me to unhook my bra. It takes three tries and almost more concentration than I have at the moment, but finally, I manage the clasp and let it fall between us.

"You trying to kill me?" His voice is a low rumble against my neck as he nuzzles under my ear.

"Just giving the fans a good show." I rock my hips and give him what I hope is a slow, sexy smile.

A growl vibrates through his chest. “By fans, you must mean me. And only me.”

“I do.” I capture his mouth in a searing kiss, all tongue and teeth and pent up desire.

His hands slide up my back, calloused fingers tickling the sensitive skin. I moan into his mouth, arching into his touch. We’re all hungry lips and wandering hands, the rest of the world fading away until there’s only Cole, only this moment, only the intense throbbing between my legs.

My hands wander over the plains of his back and shoulders as his mouth leaves a trail of scorching heat down my neck. I moan, my body yearning and squirming in anticipation, and I gasp when he takes one nipple into his mouth, teasing the other between his fingers.

“Cole, please,” I purr, writhing against him. His erection presses against my core, and I ache with a need only he can eliminate.

He lifts his head, eyes dark with desire. “Tell me what you want, sweetheart.”

“You,” I whisper. “I want you. Forever.”

I lift off of him and settle on the bed, but my attempt to wriggle out of my panties has them rolled up around my thighs.

“Here, let me help you.” But as he reaches over and hooks a thumb in the twisted fabric, he freezes and his brows draw together. “Macy, are you sure you want to do this?”

A giddy laugh escapes me, and I lick my parched lips and lift my ass up to encourage him to continue with my underwear. “Why not?”

“Your...um, what did you call it? Your policy.”

His thoughtfulness cuts through my muddled brain, and I can’t help but smile. “I think I can make an exception for my *fiancé*. If,” I add, a moment of clarity shining through the tipsy haze, “you use protection.”

"Don't worry." He leans over and plants a tender kiss on my forehead, his lips lingering. "I'm prepared—for now."

I file away the thought for later, and after tossing my panties against the wall, Cole rolls on a condom and settles on top of me. His weight is a welcome pressure as he pins me with a hand on either side of my head and his hips create a delicious sensation between my legs.

"Cole," I moan, arching into him. The feel of his bare chest against mine is intoxicating, all hard muscle and heated skin.

A low growl rumbles in his chest as one hand snakes down to find my slick folds, stroking and teasing until I'm writhing against him.

"So wet for me," he murmurs against my lips. "You feel so good."

His mouth descends to my neck, sucking and nipping as he enters me with a hard thrust. I cry out and tilt my hips to take him deeper and cling to his shoulders.

He moves slow and deep, but it's not enough, not nearly enough. I need more and tell him so, wriggling beneath him as my entire being is focused on the sensation of his length inside me.

He picks up the pace, pounding into me as our kisses turn feverish. The coil of pleasure in my belly tightens with each thrust, and crying out his name, I shatter, my fingernails digging into his flesh.

Cole thrusts erratically, chasing his own release, and spills inside me with a groan. We stay joined for a long moment, foreheads pressed together and breaths mingling while our heartbeats slow.

With a soft groan, Cole slides out of me and pads to the bathroom. I stare at the ceiling, trying to figure out if the room is spinning or if it's just me. I give up and close my eyes and just lie there, content as I've ever been, until a warm weight sinks down next to me on the bed and draws me to him. I curl against his chest, listening to the steady beat of his heart.

His fingers brush lazy patterns up and down my spine, and although we're enveloped in our own little world, noise from outside, from other trailers, here in the lot for day two of the festival tomorrow, filters in.

I nestle closer and trace patterns on the bare skin of Cole's chest as I think about our journey together. "Just like that first night, huh?"

"Not even close," he says, pressing a kiss to the top of my head. "Tonight was a million times better because you're mine."

Epilogue | Cole | The Next Morning

A RAY OF SUNSHINE streams in through the gap between the blackout shade and the windowsill. I wake and freeze for an instant until Macy rolls over and snuggles against me with a sigh, her head on my shoulder and her bare leg thrown over mine.

I draw her closer and inhale deeply, filling my lungs. She'll be up soon enough, now that it's morning, but I want to enjoy this quiet moment and thank my lucky stars. I've woken up in this bus thousands of times, but that morning, in December in Charlotte, when Macy was at my side sound asleep, just like now, was a morning I'll never forget. If I shut my eyes, I can picture it perfectly, and I know in the future, when I'm thinking back, I'll remember this moment just as clearly.

So much has changed in the seven months since the day we met, especially in the last twenty-four hours. I still can't believe this alluring woman, caring mother, and talented musician is mine. I press a kiss to her head, her long dark hair splayed out on my pillow while sounds from outside the bus, outside our cozy cocoon, break the silence.

Macy draws a deep breath. Her eyes flutter open and meet mine.

"Good morning," I murmur.

"Morning," she replies with a yawn as she stretches from head to toe and settles back against me.

I lift her hand on my chest and intertwine my fingers with hers, a flicker of pleasure coursing through me at the sparkling diamond on her finger.

"You really know how to make a girl's dreams come true, don't you, Cole Heartwood?"

I run my thumb along her knuckle. "You made my dreams come true last night and this morning."

"This morning?"

"When I woke up here, in Kissing Springs, and you were still by my side. And wearing my ring."

She's quiet for a moment. "You know what's funny?" she says. "You're technically my fiancé. I've never even really had a boyfriend, and now, here I am engaged. Once you make up your mind to commit to something, you really go all in, don't you?"

"We could be in Vegas by this afternoon and married by tonight."

Her face breaks out into a wide grin, and she slaps my chest. "We can't get married today, although that really would make it official and public, wouldn't it?"

"You tell me where and when, and I'll be there."

Her expression transforms, and I can see the exposure she's still so new to, the pressure you feel when every move you make is newsworthy, appearing in her eyes like storm clouds moving in.

I press my forehead to hers, willing her to believe what I'm about to say. "Macy Porter, our relationship is between you and me, and we're all that matters. I don't care what anyone else says or thinks or believes. I'm willing to do whatever it takes to prove to you every day how much I love you. I'm in this one thousand percent. You are my priority above everything else, including my career. You and Mason are my world now and—"

She cuts me off with a kiss. "I believe you; I do," she murmurs against my lips. "Plus," she says, lying back with a devilish grin, "You may have been a magic bullet for my career, but after you release that song you sang to me last night, you'll have another number one on the charts, no doubt."

"You think?"

She nods. "It was perfect."

I've never tried to please anyone besides myself with my music, but her praise floods my chest with warmth and love, and I realize how much I've changed since I met her. Suddenly, satisfying Macy's ear as well as her body is a priority I welcome from this day forward.

With a resigned sigh, she adds, "Plus, I can't get married today. I have plans. Mason and I are scheduled to fly back to Nashville."

Her tone tells me all I need to know.

"That doesn't sound nearly as much fun as sticking around a little bit longer. You know I never have had the chance to see Kissing Springs."

"Really?" Macy lifts her head to meet my eyes, a bright look filling her beautiful face.

"Of course." I would say more but bite my tongue. I want to explore Macy's hometown and enjoy a few more days together before it's back to Nashville, but I have an ulterior motive, too. One I'm not quite ready to share with my fiancée just yet.

She rolls over, and her back faces mine as she snuggles on my bicep and weaves her fingers through the fingers on my outstretched arm. "That sounds perfect."

I shift to spoon her, my erection pressing into her ass, and nuzzle her neck. She wiggles her bottom against my cock, and my lips curve into a smile. "But first, how about you just lie back and relax?"

A hum purrs from her chest. "I'll never say no to that, but give me a minute to freshen up, will you?"

"Take all the time you need."

Macy leans over for a quick kiss and then rises and pads out to the bathroom in the hallway, naked.

I run a hand down my stubble and stare at the ceiling with a content sigh. Then I reach for my phone on the nightstand and dismiss all the notifications on my home screen. I shoot off a text to Tessa.

I want to buy some land and build a house in Kissing Springs. Tell no one. We can talk more next week.

I hit send and set aside the phone, a ridiculous grin filling my face as I consider my surprise...and all the ways to please my fiancée when she returns.

DEAR READER, THANK YOU so much for reading **Sunshine & Sass**! I hope you enjoyed Macy & Cole's story as much as I enjoyed writing it.

If you missed Hannah & Hunter in **Scorching Santa** be sure to grab that now!

Curious to see Tessa & Tanner's love story? **Bourbon & Bets** is next up.

xoxo ~ Ellen

He checked all the boxes for a one night stand... tall, dark, rugged, and—most importantly—a stranger I'd never see again.

Until the next morning, when I find out I'm now his boss.

Tessa

Dinner and drinks with the girls to celebrate my promotion is the plan until I lock eyes with a well-built stranger across the bar—one whose dark eyes and southern drawl have me revising the schedule.

But what's the harm in having a little fun with this small town visitor? It's not like our paths will ever cross again after tonight.

Until they do.

Tanner

Combining business and pleasure is never a good idea, especially when you have no clue that's exactly what you're doing.

I'm enjoying a rare night on the town to celebrate my birthday when a curvy spitfire with an irresistible smile across the bar has me ordering another round—and inviting her back to my room in no time.

But in the morning she's vanished and I'm late for a meeting to sign the largest contract in my small construction company's history.

The only problem is... she's the new project manager in charge of the build and the one who gets to call the shots from here on out.

Read **Bourbon & Bets** today!

Also By Ellen Brooks

Welcome to **Ravish Ridge**, where sexy, small town heroes fall fast and work hard to satisfy the sassy women who capture their heart in an instant.

If you love blindsided men, women who know what they want, and steamy, small town romances, the **It Only Takes ONE** series is perfect for you. There is no cheating and no cliffhangers, just a sweet and steamy HEA for every couple.

One Shot with the Soldier
One Oath by the Officer
One Hassle for the Handyman
One Challenge for the Cowboy
One Favor from the Firefighter
One Question for the Quarterback

Holidates Series

My Sexy Holidate | Snowflakes & Holidates

My Handsome Holidate | Valentines & Holidates

Man of the Month Club

Flirt Like a Fool

Seduce Like a Siren

Welcome to Kissing Springs

Scorching Santa

Sunshine & Sass

Bourbon & Bets

Well-Matched Series

Learning His Lesson

Finding His Forever

The Scots

Falling for a Star

Tempted by the Scot

Visit www.ellenbrooks.info for all the links and to sign up for my newsletter so you won't miss a single thing.

About the Author

Ellen Brooks believes in love at first sight, eating cake for breakfast, and staying up way too late.

She's a classically trained pastry chef who now spends her days whipping up sexy and satisfying modern day love stories.

When she's not dreaming up her next characters, or plotting a happily ever after, you'll find her absorbed in a book, relaxing into shavasana, or downing a caffè americano. Oh, and belting out the lyrics to Hamilton.

Ellen lives in the desert southwest where she still *occasionally bakes a batch of cookies for her real-life hero and two girls.

*code for not often enough, if you ask them

Ellen loves to connect with readers everywhere.

amazon.com/~/e/B092SNYDJ9

bookbub.com/authors/ellen-brooks

facebook.com/authorellenbrooks/

instagram.com/ellen__brooks/

tiktok.com/@ellen.brooks.author

Milton Keynes UK
Ingram Content Group UK Ltd.
UKHW011112280823
427620UK00004B/408